Holt Math

Minnesota Test Prep
Workbook for Grade 11

HOLT, RINEHART AND WINSTON

A Harcourt Education Company

Orlando • **Austin** • New York • San Diego • Toronto • London

ISBN 0-03-093329-3

4 5 6 7 8 9 10 018 09 08

To the Student

This book is designed to help you practice for the Minnesota Comprehensive Assessments Series II in Mathematics. The MCA-II is taken in Grade 11 and measures your proficiency in Math, Reading, and Science.

The book contains practice questions arranged by topic, and practice tests.

The practice questions are organized by content strands. There are 4 strands:

- Number Sense, Computation and Operations
- Patterns, Functions and Algebra
- Data Analysis, Statistics, and Probability
- Spatial Sense, Geometry and Measurement

Within each topic, there are several 2-page worksheets on each topic. All questions are multiple choice.

At the back of the book, the practice tests contain additional practice in each of the strands.

It is a good idea to time yourself as you work some of the practice questions in order to get used to working in a timed situation.

In addition to the practice in this book, your textbook has many opportunities to practice questions in the format of the MCA-II, as well as practice tests and test-taking strategies.

Standardized Test-Taking Strategies for Math

Test Practice

Number Sense, Computation, and Operations

Patterns, Functions, and Algebra

Data Analysis, Statistics, and Probability

Spatial Sense, Geometry, and Measurement

MN Test Prep Grade 11

MCA-II in Brief

Question Format	• Multiple Choice • Gridded Response • Constructed Response
Number of Questions (Grade 11 Mathematics)	• 43 Multiple Choice • 2 Gridded-Response • 5 Constructed Response (Extended Response)
Time Allowed (Mathematics)	Every student should be given time to attempt to answer each question. As long as a student is making progress, he or she may continue working.
Materials Needed	• Number 2 pencils with erasers • Calculators are allowed for Segments 1–4 • A MCA-II Formula sheet will be provided
Links	http://www.education.state.mn.us/mde/ Accountability_Programs/Assessment_ Testing/AssessmentsIMCA_II/MCA_II_ General_Information/index.html

Standardized Test-Taking Strategies for Math

Standardized tests, such as the MCA-II, are designed in order for you to demonstrate the content and skills you have learned. It is important to keep in mind that, in most cases, the best way to prepare for these tests is to pay close attention in class and take every opportunity to improve your mathematical, reading, and writing skills.

Tips For Taking The Test

Throughout the year

- Keep up with your homework. Homework is important practice that will help you learn the skills you need for the test. Practice will also help you answer questions more quickly, leaving more time for the difficult questions.

- Review your notes, homework, and tests on a regular basis to make sure that you maintain the skills you learned earlier in the year.

- Use flashcards to learn important formulas and vocabulary words. If you can, memorize formulas to save time on the test.

- Familiarize yourself with the format and content of the test.

- Make a timeline for reviewing materials in the time leading up to the test. Do not try to "cram" the night before the test.

- Practice without your calculator, because you may not be allowed to use a calculator on the test.

Before the test

- Be sure you are well rested.

- Eat a good breakfast.

- Be on time, and be sure that you have the necessary materials.

- Be sure to bring any assistive device that you need, such as glasses or a hearing aid.

- Try not to miss class the day before the test. Your teacher may be reviewing important content.

During the Test

- Listen to the instructions of the teacher. It's easy to miss important points that can affect your score.

- Read the directions carefully. If you do not understand a direction, raise your hand and ask for clarification immediately.

- Use your scratch paper. You are more likely to make a mistake when doing a problem in your head. You can also use your written work to help check your answer. Circle the answer and write the problem number next to your work so you can find it while you are reviewing your test.

- Read the entire question, including all answer choices, and think about your answer before you make any marks on the answer sheet.

- Fill in the circle for each answer carefully and completely. Erase any stray marks on the page. If you change an answer choice, be sure to erase completely and carefully so that you do not tear a hole in the answer sheet.

- Make sure the number on the answer document matches the question number in the test booklet.

- Don't spend too much time on any one question. If you cannot answer a question right away, fill in your best choice. If you have time at the end of the test, return to any questions you are unsure of.

- If questions contain negative wording such as NOT, read them carefully and be alert for the use of double negatives within a sentence.

- Understand the format of the test so that you can gauge your time according to what section of the test you are taking.

- If you finish early, review the test and make sure the answer sheet is filled out correctly. Remember, your first answer is usually the correct one, so don't change an answer unless you can convince yourself that your original choice is wrong. Try solving the problem in a different way to see if you get the same answer.

- DON'T STRESS! Just remember what you have learned in class, and you should do well.

Tips for Answering Multiple-Choice Questions

- If there is a figure accompanying the question, review the figure carefully. Read the labels and make sure you understand what the figure represents. Remember, a figure may not be drawn to scale.

- If there is not a figure, it may be helpful to draw one on your scratch paper using the information provided.

- Read the multiple-choice question first for its general intent and then reread it carefully, looking for words that give clues or can limit possible answers to the question.

- If possible, work the question before looking at the answer choices. Then look for your answer among the given choices. If your answer is not one of the choices, read the question again. Be sure that you understand the problem. Remember, common errors are often used to generate incorrect answer choices. Be sure you work carefully.

- Make sure you answer the question being asked. A partial answer to the question may be used as an incorrect answer choice.

- Always read **all** of the possible answer choices—even if the first one seems like the correct answer. There may be a better choice farther down in the list.

- Think of what you already know about the math topic involved and use that information to help eliminate answer choices. You can also use estimation to eliminate answer choices.

- If you cannot work the question, you may be able to substitute the answer choices back into the question to find the correct choice. Start with the middle value. If the result is too large, then substitute a smaller value. If the result is too small, then substitute a larger value.

- Never leave a question blank. There is no penalty for guessing, so always choose an answer.

- When you are finished, reread the question and the selected answer to be sure that you made the best choice and that you marked it correctly on the answer sheet.

MN Test Prep Grade 11

Strategies for Success

There are various strategies you can employ ahead of time to help you feel more confident about answering questions on math standardized tests. Here are a few suggestions:

1. VISUALS

Note the labels on the charts and graphs. For example, a scale on one axis may provide a valuable clue. Read all graphs twice.

When reading diagrams, read all labels and tick marks carefully, and read diagrams twice, also.

Label the figure with any information stated in the problem that is not in the diagram. Use the properties of the figure, for example, if it is stated that a figure is a square, you can label all the sides with the same length.

If a figure is not provided, it may be helpful to draw one. Be sure that you do not assume any information that is not included in the problem. Remember, the figure does not have to look perfect. It is only to help you understand the relationships in the problem.

2. CONCEPTS

When answering questions about math concepts, don't let a hard question stump you. You can always work with what you do know. It's possible to answer a question when you know only a part of the concept being tested.

Another strategy to help you on difficult questions is to draw or sketch out the question's concept. Often you can understand how to answer a question by listing what you know, sketching the process, and then identifying what you are supposed to solve.

If you do not understand a problem on the test, try to relate it to a problem you can solve. For example, you can substitute simpler numbers into a problem and figure out how to solve it. Then try again with the original values in the problem.

3. MATH SKILLS

To help you on the math sections of the tests, practice the skills as you are reading and discussing your textbook. For example, you could put the steps to a process in order in your mind. Also, sequencing a process can become a game you play with a friend who also has to take the test. Always ask yourself what the most important points are when studying sections. Some of the more common skills for studying math are

- **Analyzing Information**—the process of breaking something down into its parts and examining the relationships between them. Analyzing enables you to better understand the whole.

- **Sequencing**—the process of placing the steps in a process in order to better understand the steps and the process as a whole. When you analyze the sequence, you are determining what happens first, second, and so on.

- **Categorizing**—the process by which you group things together by the characteristics they have in common. Categorizing helps you to make comparisons and see differences among things.

- **Identifying Cause and Effect**—interpreting the relationships between events. A *cause* makes something happen. An *effect* is what happens as a result of the cause.

- **Comparing and Contrasting**—the process of examining situations or ideas, etc., for their similarities and differences.

- **Summarizing**—the process of taking a large amount of information and boiling it down into a short clear statement. To *summarize* a problem, you must analyze the problem to find the most important points and the supporting information.

- **Paraphrasing**—a paraphrase is a restatement of someone's ideas or words. A paraphrase is usually about as long as the original; the ideas are just expressed in simpler terms. A paraphrase question might be stated like this, "According to the passage, which of these statements is accurate?"

- **Visualizing**—visualizing helps you see processes and procedures in your mind's eye. Visualizing will help you be successful on a variety of math questions you could encounter on tests.

MN Test Prep Grade 11

4. READING MATH

First, remember that what you have learned about math can help you in answering comprehension questions on tests. Also, though, remember the following points:

- Read the problem as if you were not taking a test.

- Look at the big picture. Ask yourself questions like, *What is the question being asked? What do the diagrams or graphs tell me?*

- Read the problem quickly first. This technique will help you know what information to look for as you read.

- Reread the problem and underline information related to the questions.

- Go back to the question and try to answer it in your mind before looking at the answers.

- Read all the answer choices and eliminate the ones that are obviously incorrect.

- If you can eliminate certain answers, getting the choice down to two, go ahead and pick one of the two responses. That's an educated guess, and you are most likely better off making the choice.

Analyzing Word Problems

Many students who are comfortable with basic skill problems are still stumped by word problems. These steps will help you work through word problems on standardized tests.

Step 1 Understand the problem

Read the problem carefully and make sure you understand what is being asked. You may wish to rewrite the question in your own words.

List the given information or circle it in your test booklet, if you are allowed to write in it. Cross out any unnecessary information.

Step 2 Make a plan

Think about similar problems you have seen in the past, and how you solved them.

Determine a strategy or strategies that you will use to solve the problem, such as drawing a diagram, working backward, finding a pattern, or other problem-solving strategies.

Step 3 Solve the problem

Solve the problem according to your plan. If the strategy you chose is not working, go back and revise. Write out all the steps on your scratch paper to avoid making careless mistakes.

Step 4 Look Back

Make sure you answered the question that was asked.

Check your answer in the words of the problem to make sure your answer is reasonable.

Make sure your answer is in the correct place on the answer document.

 MN Test Prep Grade 11

Learning Math Vocabulary

Learning vocabulary is important in order to be successful on standardized tests. During the test, you will not be able to ask the meaning of a word, and you may not be able to answer a question that contains a word you do not know.

Spend time learning vocabulary throughout the year so that you are prepared for your test when the time comes.

Identify important terms:

As you learn new concepts, keep a list of unfamiliar terms. Also, review the standards for your grade and write down any words you do not know.

Learn the meaning of each term:

Look up the meaning of each new word in your glossary. It may help to use the Vocabulary Questioning Strategies shown on the next page. Another way to learn vocabulary is by using graphic organizers like the ones shown below.

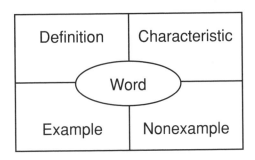 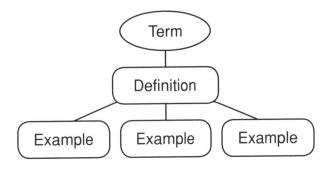

Memory aids:

Your lists of words may be used as memory aids, or it may be helpful to create flashcards with the term on the front and the definition and/or examples on the back. Review the flashcards frequently. As you learn the words, you may remove the flashcards from your stack, but keep them for occasional review before your exam.

Use context clues:

If you do encounter an unfamiliar word on your test, don't panic. Try to relate it to a familiar word or use context clues to determine the meaning of the word in the problem.

Vocabulary Questioning Strategies

Vocabulary term _____

Before you look up the word, predict its meaning. Some clues you can use are as follows:

- the way you have seen or heard the word used
- the everyday meaning of the word
- the meaning of the root word, prefix, or suffix

I think this word means _____

_____

Look up the word in your glossary, and write its meaning here.

_____

_____

Write a question in your own words that contains the vocabulary term, and write the answer.

Question: _____

_____

Answer: _____

_____

Think of a strategy to remember the meaning of the word. Some possible strategies are as follows: draw a picture that represents the word, write a poem or song about the word, or relate the math meaning to the everyday meaning of the word. Write your strategy here.

_____

_____

Math Anxiety

Math anxiety is a term used to describe fear and negative attitudes about working with numbers and taking math tests. Here are some suggestions to help alleviate math anxiety.

- Motivate yourself to learn math. Math class can be challenging, but it also has many rewards. Mathematics is a useful tool with a wide range of applications in nearly every field, as well as everyday life.

- Talk to your teacher about your anxiety. He or she may have suggestions or be able to help in other ways.

- Go to class every day! Research shows a strong correlation between attendance and math grades. Attending class should be a high priority.

- Make the most of your class time. Warm up for class by looking over the previous day's notes and homework. Write out any questions you have. If possible, read ahead in the text. Be alert and attentive. You won't get much benefit out of sleeping through class.

- Ask questions in class. If you just decide you can figure something out later, you may not understand the rest of the lecture, and fall further behind. Most often others will have the same question.

- Develop a note-taking system. If you are too busy writing every word the teacher says, you will not have time to comprehend much. Use abbreviations and shorthand during class, and re-work or re-write your notes soon after class to make sure you understand what was said.

- Do your homework as soon after class as possible. The longer you wait, the more you may forget. If you get behind, you will have a harder time understanding further material, and you may become frustrated.

- Find a study partner or group to work with. This will make math a more comfortable activity, maybe even fun!

- Find a place you are comfortable studying, where there are few distractions. If you have a certain place set aside for studying, you will find it easier to get into the right frame of mind to study there.

- Take breaks while studying. The mind works best in short periods of time, between 20 and 45 minutes. When you can't concentrate, take 5–10 minutes to walk around, stretch, or have a snack, then return to your work refreshed.

- Get help when you are stuck. Don't agonize for hours, ask your teacher, a tutor, a classmate, or a friend for help.

- Make a vocabulary list and a formula list. Use flashcards to memorize definitions and formulas. Remember, math is like a foreign language. You can't speak it if you don't know the words.

- To solidify your understanding, after you have done your homework, try the following:

  Check your answers against the answers in the back of the book.

  Do some extra problems from the book in areas you had trouble.

  Make up some practice problems and work them.

  Write out a general step-by-step procedure for solving each type of problem.

- Learn relaxation techniques and practice them before the test so that if you get frustrated you will be able to relax during the test.

- Learn more about math anxiety in books or on the Internet. Many people have math anxiety, and there are a lot of resources out there.

 MN Test Prep Grade 11

Troubleshooting

Taking practice tests can be helpful, but you will get more out of them if you analyze the tests after they have been scored to see where you made mistakes. Look at the table below to see some common types of mistakes. Use the blank rows to add in your own types with how you can avoid them in the future.

Type of mistake	Ways to avoid it in the future
I was unfamiliar with the concept involved in the question.	Review the standards to make sure I know what will be covered on the test.
I knew how to do the problem, but I couldn't remember.	Maintain skills throughout the year. Review old tests and homework to keep old topics fresh.
I misread the problem.	Read the problem carefully, and check my answer against the words of the problem to make sure the answer makes sense.
I did not know the meaning of a word in the problem.	Make lists of vocabulary terms and use vocabulary strategies to learn their meanings.
I did not transfer the answer to the answer sheet correctly.	Check frequently that the answers are in the right place. Circle the answer in the answer booklet or on scratch paper so I can go back and check it.

NUMBER SENSE, COMPUTATION, AND OPERATION

Compare and Order Real Numbers

B1 Apply the correct order of operations and grouping symbols when using calculators and other technologies.

Select the best answer for each question.

1. Which points are greater than $\frac{27}{5}$?

A. Only *H*, *K*

B. Only *H*, *M*

C. Only *T*

D. Only *M*, *T*, *R*

2. Which of the following is the smallest fraction that can be made by using pairs from the set of numbers {1, 2, 3, 4}?

A. $\frac{2}{3}$

B. $\frac{1}{3}$

C. $\frac{2}{4}$

D. $\frac{1}{4}$

Use the table to answer questions 3 to 5.

Plumber	First Hour	Price per Hour or Fraction of an Hour (after first hour)
Ant	$20	$35
Bee	$42	$27
Cat	$35	$36
Daisy	$33	$22
Elk	$40	$18

3. Which plumber charges the least for a $4\frac{1}{2}$-hour job?

A. Cat

B. Daisy

C. Bee

D. Elk

4. Which plumber is the second most expensive for 1-hour job?

A. Elk

B. Cat

C. Daisy

D. Bee

5. Which plumber charges $77 for a job that takes 3 hours?

A. Elk

B. Cat

C. Daisy

D. Bee

Name_____ Date _____ Class_____

Use the partial stock table below for questions 6 and 7.

Stock	Ticker	Div	Vol 000s	High	Low	Close
ResMed	RMD		3831	42.00	39.51	41.50
Rio Tin	RIO	2.30	168	72.75	71.84	72.74
Rockwall	ROK	1.02	6412	47.99	47.00	47.54
XYZ Co	XY		213	23.99	21.46	22.75

6. Which stock had the greatest difference between the high and low price of the day?

   A. ResMed

   B. Rio Tin

   C. Rockwall

   D. XYZ Co

7. What was the difference in volume of shares sold between the lowest closing price stock and highest closing price stock?

   A. 45000 shares

   B. 537 shares

   C. 45 shares

   D. 137,000 shares

Gridded-Response: Fill in the grid with your answer to each question.

8. Which of the following fractions is the largest? Give your answer in decimal form.

$$\frac{1}{13}, \frac{7}{17}, \frac{4}{1}, \frac{5}{5}$$

Extended-Response: Show your work for each question.

9. The following table shows elements from the periodic table.

Element	Atomic Mass (amu)	Ionic Charge
Aluminum	26.962	+3
Calcium	40.078	+2
Chlorine	35.4527	−1
Lithium	6.941	+1
Sulfur	32.066	+2

   A. Order the given elements from least to greatest atomic mass.

   B. Which subset of the real numbers (real, rational, integer, whole, natural, irrational) best describes the atomic masses of these elements?

   C. Which subset of the real numbers best describes the ionic charges of these elements?

   D. Explain why interval notation cannot be used to represent the set of atomic masses given.

NUMBER SENSE, COMPUTATION, AND OPERATION

Estimation

B1, B6 Apply the correct order of operations and grouping symbols when using calculators and other technologies. Understand that use of a calculator requires appropriate mathematical reasoning and does not replace the need for mental computation.

Select the best answer for each question.

1. A painter purchased the following items at a home store. How much did the painter spend on supplies, to the nearest dollar?

Item	Cost
wrench	$7.22
bolts	$2.89
2 gallons paint	$39.99 each
3 brushes	$4.49 each
1 pan	$2.49
2 roller covers	$4.99 each

   A. $116
   B. $102
   C. $109
   D. $62

2. Kara wants to buy a laptop computer for $895.99 and a printer for $79.99, including tax. She plans to pay for the items in 9 equal monthly payments. Which is a reasonable estimate for each payment?

   A. $9.00
   B. $80.00
   C. $100.00
   D. $110.00

3. Shea wants to purchase a rug for his bathroom. The bathroom measures 8.85 feet by 7.96 feet. Which is the best estimate of the area of the bathroom?

   A. 70.83^2 square inches
   B. 70 square inches
   C. 10,144 square inches
   D. 8.5^2 square inches

4. $30\frac{1}{4}$ square yards equal one square rod. How many square yards are 4 square rods rounded to the nearest square yard?

   A. 8 square yards
   B. 16 square yards
   C. 120 square yards
   D. 121 square yards

5. The average daily volume of a particular stock being traded on Wall Street is 765,790,333 Mil. What is this number rounded to the nearest half million?

   A. 765,000,000
   B. 770,000,000
   C. 766,000,000
   D. 767,000,000

6. Hugo qualifies for a $18,000 car loan. However, he only wants to borrow $\frac{2}{3}$ of this amount. What percent of $18,000 does Hugo want to borrow?

A. 88%

B. $66\frac{2}{3}$%

C. $33\frac{1}{3}$%

D. 23%

7. A wastewater treatment plant needs to know from each factory in the city an estimated amount of water that will be drained into the treatment plant each day. A local glue factory estimates that 337,460 gallons of water flows from their company to the treatment plant. A neighboring plant estimates that they only send one-third of the amount of water that the glue factory projects. About how many gallons of water does the neighboring plant project?

A. 110 gallons

B. 220 gallons

C. 112,487 gallons

D. 120,522 gallons

8. The estimated population in China in July 2005 was 1,306,313,812. What is one percent of this number, to the nearest hundred?

A. 13,063,100

B. 13,063,200

C. 13,064,000

D. 113,063,140

Gridded-Response: Fill in the grid with your answer to each question.

9. A brand of peanut butter is available in the following jar sizes.

Size	Cost
12 oz	$1.69
18 oz	$2\frac{11}{16}
28 oz	$3.49
40 oz	$8.79
80 oz	$9.99

One-third of the 40-ounce jar costs approximately $_____.

Extended-Response: Show your work for each question.

10. $25\frac{1}{4}$ yards equal one square rod.

How many yards are 8 square rods rounded to the nearest yard?

NUMBER SENSE, COMPUTATION, AND OPERATION

Exponents and Roots

> B1 Apply the correct order of operations and grouping symbols when using calculators and other technologies.

Select the best answer for each question.

1. Which lengths below would NOT form a right triangle?

    A. $\sqrt{3}, \sqrt{7}, 5$

    B. $\sqrt{975}, 40, 25$

    C. $2, 7, \sqrt{53}$

    D. $6, 8, 10$

2. Evaluate the expression when $x = 8$.

$$\frac{x\sqrt{(3+3)^2 + 2^3 \cdot x}}{\left(\frac{1}{2}\right)^{-1}}$$

    A. 4

    B. 24

    C. 40

    D. 80

3. What is the value of x given

    $x = \dfrac{-b \pm \sqrt{b^2 - 4ac}}{2a}$, when

    $a = 2, b = 5$ and $c = -3$?

    A. -2.5

    B. -5 or -3

    C. $\dfrac{5 \pm 2\sqrt{7}}{4}$

    D. 0.5 or -3

4. Which function is the inverse of $f(x) = x^2 - 6x + 9$ on the domain $x \geq 3$?

    A. $f^{-1}(x) = 3 + \sqrt{x}$

    B. $f^{-1}(x) = \dfrac{1}{x^2 - 6x + 9}$

    C. $f^{-1}(x) = x - 3$

    D. $f^{-1}(x) = \dfrac{1}{3 + \sqrt{x}}$

5. A single bacterium divides into 3 bacteria every hour. Assume that the same rate of division continues for 6 hours. Write a sequence that gives the number of bacteria, B, after each 1-hour period, n.

    A. $B = 3^6$

    B. $B = n^3$

    C. $B = 3^n$

    D. $B = 6^n$

6. What is the exponent on the x-term after the following expression is simplifed?

$$x^{\frac{3}{2}}\left(\sqrt{x^3}\right)^4$$

    A. 15

    B. 2

    C. $\dfrac{15}{2}$

    D. $\dfrac{7}{2}$

7. If $20 \cdot 4000 = 8 \cdot 10^x$, x equals:

   A. 4

   B. 1000

   C. 3

   D. 10

8. The formula for the distance between two points, (x_1, y_1) and (x_2, y_2) is given by the distance formula, shown below. If the distance between $(-3, 6)$ and $(x, -2)$ is $d = 4\sqrt{5}$, then the x-coordinate is _____.

$$d = \sqrt{(x_2 - x_1)^2 + (y_2 - y_1)^2}$$

   A. 1

   B. 3

   C. 5

   D. 6

9. Evaluate $\left((-3)^{-2}\right)^{-2}$.

   A. -81

   B. $-\dfrac{1}{81}$

   C. $\dfrac{1}{81}$

   D. 81

Gridded-Response: Fill in the grid with your answer to each question.

10. Simplify the expression: $\dfrac{12^{\frac{2}{3}} \cdot 12^2}{12^{-\frac{1}{3}}}$.

Extended-Response: Show your work for each question.

11. Every integer can be written as a product of powers of prime numbers, called the prime factorization of the given number.

For example, $60 = 2^2 \times 3 \times 5$

For each rational number, write the numerator and denominator by using the prime factorization of each. Then simplify the result.

   A. $\dfrac{18}{24}$

   B. $\dfrac{48}{180}$

   C. $\dfrac{250}{258}$

   D. Examine the final quotients you wrote. Explain why a prime-number base that appears in a numerator does NOT appear in the denominator, and why a prime-number base that appears in a denominator does NOT appear in the numerator.

NUMBER SENSE, COMPUTATION, AND OPERATION

Properties of Operations

> B1 Apply the correct order of operations and grouping symbols when using calculators and other technologies.

Select the best answer for each question.

1. A computer repair shop uses the function $f(t) = \sqrt{9t} + 5t^2$ to calculate their fees, where t is the number of hours they spend working on the computer. If you paid $253 to get your computer repaired, how long did the company work on repairing your computer?

   A. $t = 8.75$
   B. $t = 7.875$
   C. $t = 7.0$
   D. $t = 7.5$

2. Solve for y when $x = 8$.

   $$y = \frac{3^2 + 12x - x^2}{x^{-\frac{x}{2}}}$$

   A. 166,852
   B. 167,936
   C. 147,552
   D. 98,544

3. The day after payday you have $300. Eight days after payday, you have $146. At what average rate are you spending?

   A. $19 per day
   B. $23 per day
   C. $19.85 per day
   D. $19.25 per day

4. Solve for n.

   $$\sqrt{8262} = \sqrt{17n^2 + (2n)^2 + \left(\sqrt{9n}\right)^4}$$

   A. 10
   B. 9
   C. 8.5
   D. 9.5

5. Bank A offers a 2% annual interest rate for deposits greater than $5000. How much money will Henry have after 5 years given that he put in $5500 in year one? Round your answer to the nearest cent.

   A. $8667.00
   B. $6072.44
   C. $6627.54
   D. $6157.88

6. Luis has to simplify the following expression on a test.

   $$\frac{2^{(3-1)} \cdot (3-1)}{2}$$

   What is his second step?

   A. Compute $3 - 1$.
   B. Compute 2^2.
   C. Compute $2 \div 2$.
   D. Compute 4×3.

Name_____ Date _____ Class_____

7. The function $y = 21,300(1.34^x)$ models the population of a community x years from now. What is the most accurate prediction for the population of a community 10 years from now? Round to the nearest whole number.

A. 397,582
B. 397,587
C. 397,583
D. 244,510

8. Solve for y when $x = -2$.

$$y = x^3 + 2x - 2^{-x}$$

A. -8
B. -16
C. $-\frac{1}{4}$
D. 16

Gridded-Response: Fill in the grid with your answer to each question.

9. Use the order of operations to simplify.

$$8 \times (-4 - 3) \times (-2 + (-6)) + 52$$

Extended-Response: Show your work for each question.

10. Hank Aaron's last season in the Major Leagues was in 1976.

Hank Aaron's 1976 Statistics	
Base Hits	**Number**
Single (S)	56
Double (D)	8
Triple (T)	0
Home Run (H)	10

A player's total number of bases can be found using the expression $S + 2D + 3T + 4H$.

A. Use the table to find Hank Aaron's total bases for 1976.
A player's slugging average is found by dividing the total number of bases by the number of at bats.

B. Write out an equation to find Hank Aaron's slugging average. How many at bats did Hank Aaron have in 1976 if his slugging average was 0.413?

MN Test Prep Grade 11

NUMBER SENSE, COMPUTATION, AND OPERATION

Real Number Operations

B1 Apply the correct order of operations and grouping symbols when using calculators and other technologies.

Select the best answer for each question.

1. Dr. Cho has 625 milliliters of a solution to use in a chemistry class experiment. He divides the solution evenly among his 18 students. If he has 13 milliliters of the solution left after the experiment, how much of the solution did each student receive?

   A. 18 milliliters
   B. 20 milliliters
   C. 24 milliliters
   D. 34 milliliters

2. Anna earns $8.33 per hour working as a clerk at the local pharmacy. She works 33 hours per week and her deductions total $87.13 per week. What is her net pay?

   A. $54.13
   B. $187.76
   C. $192.45
   D. $274.89

3. Determine the circumference of a circle if the radius is 8.4 and $\pi = \frac{22}{7}$.

   A. 19.8
   B. 26.4
   C. 52.8
   D. 70.6

4. Determine the surface area of a sphere if the radius is $\frac{50}{22}$ and $\pi = \frac{22}{7}$.

   A. 5.2
   B. 16.2
   C. 28.6
   D. 64.9

5. The Lake Superior County Fair Board is starting a beautification project at the fair grounds. The Fair Board has set aside 3 areas around the grounds for beautification. Eight clubs have agreed to split the cost of purchasing trees and flowering shrubs for the project. Each area will need 12 trees and 42 flowering shrubs. If trees are $102.99 and flower shrubs are $24.99, how much will each club donate?

   A. $210.62
   B. $303.41
   C. $578.25
   D. $857.05

MN Test Prep Grade 11

6. For a class science project, Tracie is keeping track of how many calories she consumes for lunch. She does NOT want to consume more than 750 calories for lunch. The table shows the calories of some food items offered during lunch.

Item	Calories
Pizza (per slice)	650
Hamburger	410
French Fries	450
Beef Burrito	440
Bagel	310
Juice	120
Milk	50
Fresh Apple	44

Tracie bought one beef burrito, one juice, one bagel, and one fresh apple. How many calories over her limit did Tracie consume?

A. 0 calories

B. 164 calories

C. 204 calories

D. 364 calories

7. Clara purchased a new drum set on an installment plan. She made a down payment of $218.50 and then made 12 monthly payments of $87.34 each. How many dollars could she have saved if she had paid $999 in cash?

A. $0

B. $49.08

C. $1266.58

D. $267.58

Gridded-Response: Fill in the grid with your answer to each question.

8. Seven times a number increased by five, and then divided by five equals 141. Find the number.

Extended-Response: Show your work for each question.

Use the table for questions 9 and 10.

Deer Creek Nightly Cabin Rates		
	1 Bedroom	**2 Bedrooms**
June	$75	$125
July	$220	$320
August	$190	$250
$7.50 per night discount if paid in full at time of reservation.		

9. A family reserves a 1-bedroom cabin and a 2-bedroom cabin at Deer Creek. The reservations are for 1 week and 4 days in August. The family pays in advance for the cabins. How much is the total fee for the cabins?

10. The Neuw family reserves a 2-bedroom cabin at Deer Creek for 8 consecutive nights; 4 nights in June and 4 in July. If they pay in full at the time of their reservation, how much is their bill?

NUMBER SENSE, COMPUTATION, AND OPERATION

Classify Real Numbers

B1, B6 Apply the correct order of operations and grouping symbols when using calculators and other technologies. Understand that use of a calculator requires appropriate mathematical reasoning and does not replace the need for mental computation.

Select the best answer for each question.

1. Which inequality is false?

   A. $\sqrt{0.25} > 10^{-5}$

   B. $\sqrt{6} < \dfrac{5}{2}$

   C. $\dfrac{5}{9} > \dfrac{11}{20}$

   D. $9 < \sqrt{65}$

2. Which point is closest to the location of $\sqrt[3]{90}$?

   A. *H*

   B. *K*

   C. *M*

   D. *T*

3. What is the fractional equivalent of 0.125?

   A. $\dfrac{1}{12}$

   B. $\dfrac{1}{10}$

   C. $\dfrac{1}{8}$

   D. $\dfrac{1}{4}$

4. Which of the following is NOT an irrational number?

   A. $\sqrt{\pi}$

   B. 2.33215

   C. 1.2445834...

   D. $\left(\sqrt{2}\right)^{7}$

5. Which number is a rational number but NOT an integer?

   A. $\dfrac{\sqrt{16}}{2}$

   B. $\dfrac{\left(\sqrt[3]{125}\right)^{2}}{5}$

   C. $\dfrac{\sqrt{64}}{32}$

   D. $\left(\dfrac{350}{70}\right)^{2}$

6. Which of the following is the greatest integer less than 460,000 that can be written using all of the digits from 1 through 6?

   A. 452,136

   B. 451,326

   C. 456,321

   D. 461,236

7. Which number has the greatest absolute value?

   A. $10\frac{2}{3}$

   B. $\sqrt{65}$

   C. $-\frac{3^4}{2}$

   D. $-\frac{10(4.5)^{-4}}{3^{-2}}$

8. Which of these numbers belongs to all of the following sets: whole, integer, rational, real?

   A. $\sqrt{\frac{196}{49}}$

   B. $\sqrt{\frac{10}{7}}$

   C. $-\frac{43}{5}$

   D. $\sqrt{\frac{24}{8}}$

9. What type of number is $\left(15\sqrt{36}\right)^3$?

   A. rational

   B. irrational

   C. rational, natural, whole

   D. rational, natural

10. What would have to be true about a, b and x if $\frac{ax}{b}$ is irrational?

    A. a, b, and x must all be irrational

    B. either a or b or x must be irrational

    C. a and b must all be rational

    D. none of the above

11. If x cannot be written as $\frac{a}{b}$, where a and b are integers, then x is:

    A. $\frac{3}{7}$

    B. 0.5

    C. $\sqrt{\frac{3}{2}}$

    D. 2

Gridded-Response: Fill in the grid with your answer to each question.

12. Find a real number between 3.14 and $\frac{23}{7}$.

Extended-Response: Show your work for each question.

13. A. What is the difference between a rational number and an irrational number.

    B. List all the irrational number you know between 1 and 10.

MN Test Prep Grade 11

NUMBER SENSE, COMPUTATION, AND OPERATION

Scientific Notation

B2 Know, use and translate calculator notational conventions to mathematical notation.

Select the best answer for each question.

1. The gross profit of an educational publishing company for the past two years was 4.57 billion dollars. What is this value in scientific notation?

 A. $\$4.57 \times 10^8$

 B. $\$4.57 \times 10^9$

 C. $\$4.57 \times 10^{11}$

 D. $\$4.57 \times 10^{12}$

2. Which of these numbers is written in scientific notation?

 A. 85.6×10^2

 B. $8.56 + 10^2$

 C. 8.56×10^2

 D. 8.10^2

3. The size of a certain organism is 0.0000425 mm long. What is the size of the organism written in scientific notation?

 A. 4.25×10^{-5} mm

 B. 4.25×10^{-6} mm

 C. 4.25×10^{-7} mm

 D. 4.25×10^5 mm

4. A drop of water contains about 1.7×10^{21} water molecules. How many water molecules are there in a glass of water that has 2.5×10^4 drops?

 A. 1.47×10^{-17}

 B. 2.89×10^{42}

 C. 4.25×10^{25}

 D. 5.25×10^8

5. China's population in 2001 was approximately 1,273,000,000. Mexico's population for the same year was about 1.02×10^8. How much greater was China's population than Mexico's?

 A. 1,375,000,000

 B. 1.171×10^9

 C. 1,247,020,000

 D. 1.02×10^9

6. The Alpha Centauri star system is about 4.3 light-years from Earth. One light-year, the distance light travels in 1 year, is about 6 trillion miles. About how many miles away from Earth is Alpha Centauri?

 A. 2.58×10^{13}

 B. 6.00×10^{13}

 C. 1.03×10^{12}

 D. 2.58×10^9

13

7. In the fall of 2001, students in Columbia South Carolina raised $440,000 to buy a new fire truck for New York City. If the money had been collected in pennies, how many pennies would that have been?

   A. 4.4×10^6

   B. 4.4×10^5

   C. 4.4×10^7

   D. 4.4×10^8

8. The earliest rocks native to Earth formed during the Archean eon. This eon extended from 3,800 million years ago to 2,500 million years ago. Calculate the length of this eon.

   A. 1.3×10^8 years

   B. 1.3×10^9 years

   C. 1.83×10^9 years

   D. 1.83×10^8 years

Gridded-Response: Fill in the grid with your answer to each question.

9. In correct scientific notation what is the power on ten of the quotient of $(3.18 \times 10^7) \div (3.25 \times 10^{-3})$?

Extended-Response: Show your work for each question.

10. Astronomers measure distances within our solar system in astronomical units (AU). 1 AU $\approx$ 92,956,000 mi or 149,600,000 km (the distance from the Earth to the Sun)

Planet	km	Scientific Notation	AU
Mercury	57,900,000		
Venus	108,200,000		
Earth	149,600,000		
Mars	227,900,000		
Jupiter	778,400,000		

The table gives each planet's mean distance from the Sun in kilometers. Write these distances in scientific notation. Convert to AUs by dividing each planet's mean distance from the Sun by 1.496×10^8. Round your answers to the nearest tenth of an AU.

PATTERNS, FUNCTIONS, AND ALGEBRA

Algebraic Expressions

B1, B12 Translate among equivalent forms of expressions, such as, simplify algebraic expressions involving nested pairs of parentheses and brackets, simplify rational expressions, factor a common term from an expression, and apply associative, commutative and distributive laws. Understand how slopes can be used to determine whether lines are parallel or perpendicular. Given a line and a point not on the line, find the equations for the lines passing through that point and parallel or perpendicular to the given line.

Select the best answer for each question.

1. The length, ℓ, of a rectangle is 5 more than twice the width, w, of a rectangle. Which expression best describes the length of the rectangle?

   A. $5 - \dfrac{1}{2}w$

   B. $5 + \dfrac{1}{2}w$

   C. $5 + 2w$

   D. $5 - 2w$

2. In $-22j + 13b$, which relationship between j and b is true?

   A. j is dependent on b.

   B. j and b are independent of each other.

   C. b is dependent on j.

   D. There is no relationship between j and b.

3. Solve for n given that $7n - \dfrac{6}{5}n$ equals $3 + \dfrac{1}{6}n$.

   A. $n = \dfrac{90}{169}$ **C.** $n = \dfrac{80}{173}$

   B. $n = \dfrac{7}{30}$ **D.** $n = 4$

4. Simplify the following.

   $$\frac{1}{3}(2x + 6y)$$

   A. $\dfrac{2}{3}x + y$

   B. $x + \dfrac{4}{3}y$

   C. $\dfrac{2}{3}x - \dfrac{4}{3}y$

   D. $\dfrac{2}{3}x + 2y$

5. What is value of the expression if $x = 5$?

   $$3x^x\left(\frac{3}{5}x + 2^x\right) - |x|$$

   A. 440,625

   B. 318,779

   C. 328,120

   D. 438,710

MN Test Prep Grade 11

Name_____ Date _____ Class_____

6. Simplify the following:

$$\frac{3\left(\sqrt[3]{\frac{(-2)^2}{9}}\right)^3}{-2}$$

A. $-\dfrac{8}{3}$

B. $-\dfrac{2}{3}$

C. $-\dfrac{5}{6}$

D. $\dfrac{13}{6}$

7. At the Beyond Harmony spa, it costs $35 per half an hour for a Swedish massage plus an $8 fee for the soothing oils and lotions. What is the total for an hour and 45 minute massage?

A. $43.50

B. $75.50

C. $130.50

D. $161.00

8. Solve the matrix equation for b.

$$\begin{pmatrix} 4+a & b+5 \\ c+2 & 2d \end{pmatrix} = \begin{pmatrix} -7 & -2 \\ 3 & -8 \end{pmatrix}$$

A. -11

B. -7

C. -3

D. 2

Gridded-Response: Fill in the grid with your answer to each question.

9. Four times a number decreased by four, and then divided by five equals 40. Find the number.

Extended-Response: Show your work for each question.

10. A. Write an expression that is equivalent to the following:

$$\left(\frac{p^{-1}q^{-2}}{p^{-1}}\right)^{-4}\left(\left(\frac{-p^5q^{-3}}{p^{-3}q^{-1}}\right)^{-3}p^2\right)$$

B. What would be the value of the expression if p is 1 and q is 0?

11. Explain how to determine the equivalency of expressions.

MN Test Prep Grade 11

PATTERNS, FUNCTIONS, AND ALGEBRA

Linear Functions

B3, A3, B7 Find equations of a line given two points on the line, a point and the slope of the line, or the slope and the *y*-intercept of the line. Analyze the effects of coefficient changes on linear and quadratic functions and their graphs. Solve linear equations and inequalities in one variable with numeric, graphic, and symbolic methods. Translate among equivalent forms of expressions, such as, simplify algebraic expressions involving nested pairs of parentheses and brackets, simplify rational expressions, factor a common term from an expression, and apply associative, commutative and distributive laws.

Select the best answer for each question.

1. Which two of these lines will never intersect?
   I $y = 15x + 15$
   II $y = 10x + 15$
   III $y = 15x + 10$
   IV $y = 15x + 15$

   A. I and IV
   B. I and II
   C. I and III
   D. II and III

2. Which of the following linear equations represents the following arithmetic sequence?

   5, 9, 13, 17, 21, 25

   A. $y = 4x + 1$
   B. $y = 4x + 4$
   C. $y = 4x + 5$
   D. $y = 5x$

3. Which of the following equations represents the line with the slope that is greatest in magnitude?

   A. $y = 2x - 5$
   B. $10x = y + 45$
   C. $3y = 9x - 27$
   D. $18y + 36x = 5$

4. What is $f(8)$ in the following equation?

   $$f(x) = 2x - 15$$

   A. −11
   B. 11
   C. −1
   D. 1

5. Two lines are NOT parallel. What does this tell us?

   A. They have different slopes and *y*-intercepts
   B. They have different slopes
   C. They have the same slope
   D. They have different intercepts

6. Which function is the inverse of $f(x) = x - 3$?

   A. $f^{-1}(x) = x + 3$
   B. $f^{-1}(x) = \frac{1}{3}x$
   C. $f^{-1}(x) = -\frac{1}{3}x$
   D. $f^{-1}(x) = 3x$

7. What is the slope of the line that passes through the points (3, 1) and (6, 10)?

A. 3   **C.** $\dfrac{1}{3}$

B. −3   **D.** $-\dfrac{1}{3}$

8. Which of these functions is linear?

A. $y = x\cos x$

B. $y = 5^{x+1}$

C. $5y - 3x = 5x + 7x + 137$

D. $2y = 8x^3 - 4$

9. What is the *y*-intercept of the following equation?

$$y + 4 = 5x + 6 + 2x$$

A. 10   **C.** −4

B. 2   **D.** 6

10. Mr. Walter made each of his 14 grandchildren a set of building blocks. Each set had 20 rectangular pieces, 15 cubes, 6 triangular pieces, and 3 cylinders. What was the total number of blocks in all the sets?

A. 44   **C.** 616

B. 58   **D.** 812

11. Which of the operations, +, −, × or ÷, should be placed in the expression, −4 __ 5 __ 2 __ 3^2 so that the value is −27?

A. −, −, ×

B. +, −, ×

C. ÷, −, +

D. +, ÷, −

12. What is the first step in simplifying the following expression?

$$\left(\dfrac{-8}{3\sqrt{\dfrac{16}{9}}} \right)^2$$

A. Square −8.

B. Find the square root of $\dfrac{16}{9}$.

C. Multiply 3 and 16.

D. Divide 9 by 3.

Gridded-Response: Fill in the grid with your answer to each question.

13. In the table, what is the value of *m*?

x	y
0	m
1	12
2	15
3	18
4	21

Extended-Response: Show your work for each question.

14. Coordinates $C(4, 6)$ and $D(8, 22)$ are connected by a line.

A. What is the equation of this line?

B. Sketch the graph of this line.

C. What is the equation of a parallel line passing through $(2, 10)$?

D. How many points of intersection will these two lines have?

E. If you double the slope of the first line, will this change your answer to part D? Explain.

MN Test Prep Grade 11

Name_____ Date _____ Class_____

PATTERNS, FUNCTIONS, AND ALGEBRA

Patterns, Sequences, and Functions

B9, B10 Use appropriate terminology and mathematical notation to define and represent recursion. Create and use recursive formulas to model and solve real-world and mathematical problems.

Select the best answer for each question.

1. The ordered pairs shown form a quadratic pattern.

x	y
0	5
−1	7
−2	13
−3	23
−4	?
−5	55

What is the missing *y*-value?

A. 25

B. 28

C. 35

D. 37

2. Which polynomial does NOT follow the same pattern as the other polynomials?

A. $x^2 - 6x + 9$

B. $4x^2 - 12x + 9$

C. $9x^2 - 6x + 1$

D. $16x^2 - 12x + 9$

3. Which sequence is best described by the graph?

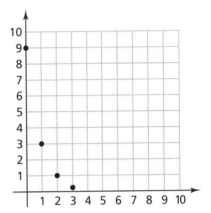

A. $t_n = \frac{1}{3}n + 9$ C. $t_n = \left(\frac{1}{3}\right)^{-n}$

B. $t_n = 9\left(\frac{1}{3}\right)^n$ D. $t_n = 3\left(\frac{1}{3}\right)^n$

4. Christa arranged chairs for seating at an outdoor concert. There were 11 rows. Two chairs were in the first row and the other rows each had 5 more chairs than the row before it. How many chairs were there in total?

A. 52

B. 68

C. 113

D. 297

5. Study the pattern below. Which choice gives the next three terms of this pattern?

A c E F h J K m O P r T

A. U w Y

B. v W z

C. V w x

D. u X z

6. Describe how the terms change in the following sequence.

2, 6, 22, 58, 122 ...

A. The terms increase by consecutive even numbers.

B. The terms increase by multiples of 2.

C. The terms increase by squares of consecutive odd numbers.

D. The terms increase by squares of consecutive even numbers.

7. What is the fifth term of a geometric sequence with a second term of 27 and a common ratio of 3?

A. 90

B. 688

C. 243

D. 729

Gridded-Response: Fill in the grid with your answer to each question.

8. A population growth curve is an exponential relationship that plots the population of bacteria versus the time. For a particular species, there are originally 2 bacteria in the population. Every minute the population triples. Using this model how many bacterium would there be at $t = 5$?

Extended-Response: Show your work for each question.

9. Describe how the terms change in the following sequence.

4, 13, 38, 87, ...

10. Jamie's parents deposit money into her bank account every month. In January, they deposited $50. In February, they deposited $100. In March, they deposited $200. Jamie says that she should receive $400 for April. Her parents said that she should be given $350. Who is correct?

PATTERNS, FUNCTIONS, AND ALGEBRA

Quadratic Equations

A1, A4, B8 Know the numeric, graphic, and symbolic properties of linear, step, absolute value, and quadratic functions. Graphic properties may include rates of change, intercepts, and maxima and minima. Apply basic concepts of linear, quadratic, and exponential expressions or equations in real-world problems such as loans, investments, and the path of a projectile. Find real solutions to quadratic equations in one variable with numeric, graphic, and symbolic methods.

Select the best answer for each question.

1. Is the following the quadratic formula?

$$x = \frac{b \pm \sqrt{b^2 - 4ac}}{2a}$$

   A. Yes

   B. No

   C. Cannot be determined

   D. Sometimes

2. Solve.

$$4x^2 - 10 = -13x - 7x$$

   A. $x = -10 \pm 2\sqrt{35}$

   B. $x = \dfrac{5 \pm \sqrt{35}}{2}$

   C. $x = \dfrac{-5 \pm \sqrt{140}}{2}$

   D. $x = \dfrac{-5 \pm \sqrt{35}}{2}$

3. Factor fully. $8x^2 - 2x - 3$

   A. $(4x + 1)(2x + 2)$

   B. $(4x - 3)(2x + 1)$

   C. $(2x + 2)(3x + 2)$

   D. $(4x - 1)(2x + 3)$

4. Expand. $(7x + 6)(5x + 3)$

   A. $35x^2 + 33x + 18$

   B. $35x^2 + 51x + 18$

   C. $7x^2 + 51x + 15$

   D. $35x^2 - 51x + 18$

5. What is the solution set for the equation $\dfrac{x}{x + 3} + \dfrac{2}{x} = \dfrac{5}{2x}$?

   A. $\{-3, 0\}$

   B. $\left\{-1, 1\frac{1}{2}\right\}$

   C. $\left\{-3, \frac{1}{2}\right\}$

   D. $\left\{-1\frac{1}{2}, 1\right\}$

6. If the equation $w = -4x^2 + 11x + 3$ models an animal's weight in x days after it is born, is it physically reasonable to discuss $w(17)$?

   A. Yes

   B. No

   C. Cannot be determined

   D. Sometimes

7. What are the solutions for this equation:

$$x^2 - x - 12 = 0$$

A. −3 and 4

B. −3 and 5

C. −2 and −4

D. −0.205 and −14.795

8. If $y = x^2 + 8x + 16$, what is the vertex?

A. (4, 0)

B. (−4, 0)

C. (4, 4)

D. (8, 16)

Gridded-Response: Fill in the grid with your answer to each question.

9. Jones likes to collect stamps. The equation $b = 3(-2x + 8)^2$ models this habit, where b is the number of stamps collected for the day and x is the number of days after she started collecting. What value for x will result in the minimum value for b?

Extended-Response: Show your work for each question.

10. Complete the square for this equation and put the answer in vertex form.

$$y = x^2 + 16x + 70$$

11. A rock is falling from the top of a building. Its velocity is modeled by the equation $v = 4.9t^2$, where v is the velocity in meters per second and t is the time in seconds. What will be the rock's velocity 100 seconds after it is dropped.

12. A certain type of bacteria has the following model to represent its population during an experiment: $p = t^2 + 14t + 5$, where p is the population in thousands and t is the time in hours. How many bacteria will be in the experiment 10 hours after it started?

PATTERNS, FUNCTIONS, AND ALGEBRA

Quadratic Functions

A4, A1 B8 Know the numeric, graphic, and symbolic properties of linear, step, absolute value, and quadratic functions. Graphic properties may include rates of change, intercepts, and maxima and minima. Apply basic concepts of linear, quadratic, and exponential expressions or equations in real-world problems such as loans, investments, and the path of a projectile. Find real solutions to quadratic equations in one variable with numeric, graphic, and symbolic methods.

Select the best answer for each question.

1. Is the following a quadratic function problem?

   "Jim is standing behind Tom. They walk in opposite direction on a straight walkway for 10 minutes and then walk back until they stand side by side again. Suppose they both walk at a constant speed, what function can represent the distance between them treating time as the independent variable?"

   A. Yes
   B. No
   C. Sometimes
   D. It cannot be determined.

2. Which of the following is a parabola that opens to the side?

   A. $y = \frac{1}{2}x^2$

   B. $x = -\frac{2}{3}y^2$

   C. $x = \frac{1}{2}y^2$

   D. Both B and C are correct.

3. Which of the following is a quadratic function?

   A.

Input	1	2	4	4
Output	1	2	3	4

   B.

Input	0	3	6	9
Output	5	15	20	25

   C.

Input	4	3	2	1
Output	−1	0	1	4

   D. None of the above

4. The equation $h = 2t^2 - 55t + 50$ gives the height h of a ball from the ground t seconds after the ball was thrown. Is this a good model for the first few seconds?

   A. Yes, it opens up.
   B. No, it opens up.
   C. Yes, it opens down.
   D. No, it opens down.

5. What would be the maximum value for y given that $y = -3(x-5)^2 + 14$?

   A. 14
   B. 70
   C. 13
   D. 3

6. Is $c = 60\sqrt{x}$ a quadratic function?

   A. Yes

   B. No

   C. It cannot be determined.

   D. Sometimes

7. Jimmy gets $1 on day one from his mother, $4 on day two, $9 on day three, and $16 on day four, etc. What function can model this situation?

   A. Quadratic only

   B. Linear only

   C. Exponential only

   D. Both quadratic and cubic

8. Determine whether the point (4, 9) is located on the graph $y = x^2 - 2x + 1$.

   A. Yes, the point is on the graph.

   B. The point is not on the graph.

   C. There is not enough information.

   D. The graph passes through the point more than once.

9. What is the degree of a quadratic function?

   A. 1

   B. 2

   C. 3

   D. 4

Gridded-Response: Fill in the grid with your answer to each question.

10. Katy likes to catch butterflies. The equation $b = -2(x - 4)^2 + 25$ models this habit, where b is the number of butterflies caught for the hour and x is the number of hours after she started catching. What is the maximum amount of butterflies Katy will catch?

Extended-Response: Show your work for each question.

11. The picture measures 6 inches × 8 inches. The width of the picture frame is equal all around, and is given as x.

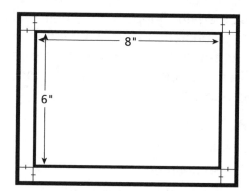

Determine a quadratic equation, in standard form, to solve in order to determine x, if the area of the picture, including the frame, is 80 square inches.

Name_____ Date _____ Class_____

PATTERNS, FUNCTIONS, AND ALGEBRA

Solve Multi-Step Equations

B5, B7 Use a variety of models such as equations, inequalities, algebraic formulas, written statements, tables and graphs, or spreadsheets to represent functions and patterns in real-world and mathematical problems. Solve linear equations and inequalities in one variable with numeric, graphic, and symbolic methods

Select the best answer for each question.

1. Which value of k is a solution to $3(5 - k) = 0$?

   A. -3

   B. 5

   C. 3

   D. -5

2. Which number is a solution to the equation $5x + 3 = 2(x - 3)$?

   A. $x = -1$

   B. $x = -2$

   C. $x = -3$

   D. $x = -4$

3. Which equation has $x = -4$ as a solution?

Equation I	**Equation II**
$14 - 3x = 2$	$4x - 3 = 13$
Equation III	**Equation IV**
$16 + 5x = -4$	$2x - 30 = -22$

   A. Equations I, III and IV

   B. Equations II and III

   C. Equations III and IV

   D. Equation III only

4. Solve for n:

$$\frac{1}{4}n - \frac{1}{8}n = 3 - \frac{1}{16}n$$

   A. $n = \dfrac{7}{3}$

   B. $n = 3$

   C. $n = \dfrac{280}{9}$

   D. $n = 16$

5. Which equation has a x-intercept of 4 and a y-intercept of -1?

   A. $4x - y = 4$

   B. $x - 4y = 4$

   C. $4x - 4y = 1$

   D. $-4x - y = -1$

6. What is the x-intercept of the line $-4x + 3y = -12$?

   A. $(-4, 0)$

   B. $(-3, 0)$

   C. $(3, 0)$

   D. $(4, 0)$

MN Test Prep Grade 11

7. For which equation is $x = \dfrac{2}{3}$ the solution?

   A. $2x - 3 = -6$

   B. $3x - 1 = 1$

   C. $4x + 1 = -5$

   D. $\dfrac{3}{2}x = \dfrac{3}{8}$

8. Solve the equation for b.

$$0.2b + 4 = 0.1(b - 10)$$

   A. $b = 0.5$

   B. $b = -50$

   C. $b = -0.5$

   D. $b = 50$

9. Which value(s) of x make(s) this equation false?

$$-3x + 12 = 0$$

   A. 3

   B. 4

   C. 5

   D. A and C

10. In the equation $p + g = 7$ which relationship between p and g is true?

   A. g is dependent on p.

   B. p is dependent on g.

   C. p and g are dependent on each other.

   D. g is always larger than p.

Gridded-Response: Fill in the grid with your answer to each question.

11. Which value of c makes this equation true?

$$5c - c + 6 = 16 - 6c$$

Extended-Response: Show your work for each question.

12. Marianne is doing a word problem that says the sum of three consecutive even numbers is 62. The equation that she sets up is $n + (n + 2) + (n + 4) = 62$. What does the expression $n + 4$ represent?

13. A rectangle has sides measuring $x + 4$ cm and $x + 5$ cm. You determine that the perimeter is 38 cm.

   A. What are the side lengths of the rectangle?

   B. Determine the area of the rectangle?

MN Test Prep Grade 11

PATTERNS, FUNCTIONS, AND ALGEBRA

Systems of Equations

B11 Solve systems of two linear equations and inequalities with two variables using numeric, graphic and symbolic methods.

Select the best answer for each question.

1. Which ordered pair represents the solution to the following linear system?

   $y = 4x - 4$
   $y = -2x + 8$

   A. $(4, 2)$
   B. $(-4, -2)$
   C. $(2, 4)$
   D. $(2, -4)$

2. Which ordered pair represents the solution to the following linear system?

   $y = 5x + 3$
   $y - x = 4x + 2$

   A. $(3, 7)$
   B. $(-3, 7)$
   C. There are infinitely many solutions
   D. No solution

3. In which case would a system of two linear equations have multiple solutions?

   A. The lines are perpendicular.
   B. The lines are parallel.
   C. The lines have the same equation.
   D. A, B, and C are all correct.

4. Which set of inequalities represents the solution to the following system of inequalities?

   $y > 2x + 2$
   $y < 3x + 3$

   A. $x > 1$
   B. $x < 1$
   C. $x > -1$
   D. $x < -1$

5. Which of the following linear systems has the solution $(4, 5)$?

   A. $y = 3x - 7$
      $y = 4x + 3$

   B. $y = 3x - 7$
      $2y - x = 3$

   C. $y = 3x + 1$
      $2y - 5x = 32$

   D. $2y = 3x - 2$
      $y - x = 1$

27

6. Which system of equations is represented by the graph shown below?

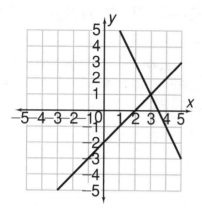

A. $x - y = 2$
$2x + y = 7$

B. $x - y = 2$
$2x - y = 7$

C. $x + y - 2$
$2x + y = -7$

D. $x + y = 2$
$2x + y = 7$

7. One electrician charges $15 per hour, as well as a $150 flat fee. A second electrician charges a $100 flat fee, and $20 per hour. At what hour would the two amounts be equal, and which electrician would be cheaper for any hours after that?

A. 5, first

B. 10, first

C. 10, second

D. 5, second

Gridded-Response: Fill in the grid with your answer to each question.

8. A CD club offers two membership plans. The first plan costs $25 per month. The second plan costs $10 per month plus $2 for each CD you rent. Which is the least number of CDs you need to buy so the first plan is worthwhile?

Extended-Response: Show your work for each question.

9. Your little brother's electronic toys require AA and AAA batteries. Save-a-Penny is having a sale and is selling packs of AA batteries for $1.89 and packs of AAA batteries for $1.53. You bought 8 packs and spent a total of $13.32.

A. Write and graph a system of linear equations to solve the problem.

B. How many packs of each kind did you buy?

MN Test Prep Grade 11

PATTERNS, FUNCTIONS, AND ALGEBRA

Transformation of Graphs and Functions

A5, A4 Apply basic concepts of linear, quadratic, and exponential expressions or equations in real-world problems such as loans, investments, and the path of a projectile. Distinguish functions from other relations using graphic and symbolic methods

Select the best answer for each question.

1. If curve 1 is $y = \frac{1}{3}x^3 + 2$, what is the equation of curve 2?

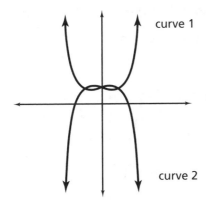

curve 1

curve 2

A. $-\frac{1}{3}x^3 + 2$

B. $-\frac{1}{3}x^3 - 2$

C. $2 + \frac{1}{3}x^3$

D. $-2 + \frac{1}{3}x^3$

One form of an exponential function is $f(x) = a2^{bx+c} + d$. Use this for questions 2−4.

2. If you wanted to shift the graph of the function vertically, what would you do?

A. change a
B. change b
C. change c
D. change d

3. If you wanted to shift the graph of the function horizontally, what would you do?

A. change a
B. change b
C. change c
D. none of the above

4. If you wanted to make the parabola narrower, what would you do?

A. change a or c
B. change b or d
C. change b
D. change d

5. To change the width of the parabola and translate it 2 units up, which of the following letters would need to be changed in the equation $y = a(x - b)^2 - c$?

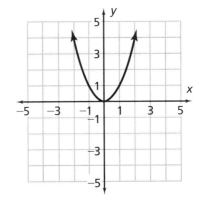

A. a and b C. a and c
B. b and c D. a, b and c

MN Test Prep Grade 11

6. How is the graph of $y = -0.5x^2$ different than the graph of $y = x^2$?

   A. All of the y values will increase.

   B. A vertical stretch by a factor of 2, and a reflection on the x-axis.

   C. A vertical compression by a factor of 0.5, and a reflection on the y-axis.

   D. A horizontal stretch by a factor of 2, and reflection on the x-axis.

7. Adding a negative constant to the beginning of the x^2 term of a quadratic function will result in:

   A. A vertical stretch

   B. A reflection on the x-axis

   C. An upward shift of the graph

   D. A vertical compression

8. How can you locate two parabolas so that they never cross each other?

   A. Shift one of them horizontally

   B. Shift one of them vertically

   C. Reflect one of them across the x-axis

   D. Both B and C are correct.

9. Is the following statement correct?

"Even degree functions do not have to cross the x-axis."

   A. Yes

   B. No

   C. Sometimes

   D. Cannot be determined

Gridded-Response: Fill in the grid with your answer to each question.

10. A polynomial with degree 5 will have no more than how many roots?

Extended-Response: Show your work for each question.

11. Given the graph of $y = x^3$, describe how you would sketch the graph of $y = 2(x - 3)^3 - 4$?

12. Sketch the graph of $y = \frac{1}{2}x^2 + 1$ given the graph of $y = x^2$ below.

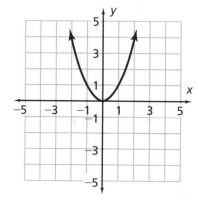

PATTERNS, FUNCTIONS, AND ALGEBRA

Model with Functions

A2,B6, A4 A5 Apply the laws of exponents to perform operations on expressions with integer exponents. Know, use and translate calculator notational conventions to mathematical notation. Apply basic concepts of linear, quadratic and exponential expressions or equations in real-world problems such as loans, investments and the path of a projectile. Distinguish functions from other relations using graphic and symbolic methods.

Select the best answer for each question.

1. Evaluate the expression.

$$6^4 \cdot \frac{1}{4} \div \left(\sqrt{15 - 9 - 2}\right)^3 - 2\frac{1}{2}$$

  A. −1.75

  B. 16

  C. 38

  D. 58.9

2. Which expression represents the verbal phrase "four times the quantity of a number and twelve"?

  A. $4(n + 12)$

  B. $4n + 12$

  C. $12 + n \cdot 4$

  D. $4 + (n + 12)$

3. Rebecca has to simplify the following expression on a test.

$$\frac{\left(22 + 6^3\right) - 5 \cdot 3 - 4^2 + 12}{3}$$

What is her second step?

  A. Compute $22 + 216$.

  B. Compute 4^2.

  C. Add 12.

  D. Compute $216 - 11$.

4. Mr. Walter made each of his 14 grandchildren a set of building blocks. Each set had 20 rectangular pieces, 15 cubes, 6 triangular pieces, and 3 cylinders. What was the total number of blocks in all the sets?

  A. 44

  B. 58

  C. 616

  D. 812

5. Tim says $4^{2t - 7} = \dfrac{1}{4^{7 - 2t}}$ when $t = 1000$. Is he correct?

  A. Yes

  B. No

  C. Cannot be determined

  D. None of the above

6. What is the first step in simplifying the following expression?

$$\left(\frac{-8}{3\sqrt{\frac{16}{9}}}\right)^2$$

  A. Square −8.

  B. Find the square root of $\dfrac{16}{9}$.

  C. Multiply 3 and 16.

  D. Divide 9 by 3.

7. The formula for finding the perimeter of a rectangle is given by $P = 2\ell + 2w$. Which statement best describes how to solve the equation for w?

 A. Subtract 2ℓ from both sides and then divide both sides by 2.

 B. Divide P by 2 and subtract 2ℓ from both sides.

 C. Divide both sides by 2ℓ.

 D. Divide both sides by 2ℓ and subtract 2 from both sides.

8. To solve the following system of equations by elimination, which step would you perform first?

$$\frac{2}{3}x + \frac{1}{4}y = 1$$

$$x + 2y = 2$$

 A. Add the two equations.

 B. Subtract the two equations.

 C. Multiply the first equation by 12.

 D. Multiply the first equation by -3

Gridded-Response: Fill in the grid with your answer to each question.

9. Suppose it costs $4.25 for the first minute of a phone call of an international phone call and $1.70 for each additional minute. The cost of the phone call can then be expressed by the formula $c = \$4.25 + 1.70(m - 1)$, where c is the total cost in dollars and m is the number of minutes. What is the cost in dollars for a call that lasts 1 hour 23 minutes?

Extended-Response: Show your work for each question.

10. What does y equal when $m = 2$ and $t = -4$? Show your steps and give an exact answer.

$$y = \sqrt{5m} + \left(3t^{\,m-t}\right)^2$$

PATTERNS, FUNCTIONS, AND ALGEBRA

Functions and Their Behavior

A5, A1, A4 Distinguish functions from other relations using graphic and symbolic methods. Know the numeric, graphic, and symbolic properties of linear, step, absolute value, and quadratic functions. Graphic properties may include rates of change, intercepts, maxima and minima. Apply basic concepts of linear, quadratic, and exponential expressions or equations in real-world problems.

Select the best answer for each question.

1. Which of the following is a linear function?

   A. $2y = 3x^2 + 7$

   B. $3y = 1^{x+1} - 7 - \frac{1}{x}$

   C. $7y = 3x + 8x - 17$

   D. All of the above

2. Which of the following is a function?

   A. $2y^2 = 3x^2 + 7$

   B. $3y = 1^{x+1} - 7 \pm \frac{1}{x}$

   C. $7y = 3x + 8x - 17 - y^2$

   D. None of the above

3. Name the model that the graph of $y = 3x^2 + 7x + 5$ represents.

   A. Quadratic

   B. Exponential Growth

   C. Exponential Decay

   D. Linear

4. A population growth curve is an exponential relationship that plots the population of bacteria versus the time. For a particular species, there are originally 2 bacteria in the population. Every minute the population triples. Using this model how many bacterium would there be at $t = 3$?

   A. 7 bacteria

   B. 17 bacteria

   C. 54 bacteria

   D. 486 bacteria

5. Which of the following statements is correct?

   A. The independent variable is on the y-axis.

   B. The dependent variable is on the x-axis.

   C. The dependent variable is on the y-axis.

   D. The dependent variable is on the y-axis or x-axis.

6. Which of the following statements is the most correct about the function $f(x) = x + 2$?

A. It is a function, but not a relation.

B. It is a relation, but not a function.

C. It is neither a function nor a relation.

D. It is both a function and a relation.

7. Which of the following functions matches the data in the table?

x	y
0	2
2	5
4	8
6	11

A. $y = 1.5x + 2$

B. $y = 3x$

C. $y = 3x^2 - 3x + 2$

D. $y = 3x + 2$

8. A demand-price curve is a linear relationship that plots the expected price of an item versus the expected number sold. For a particular item, a price of $4.50 is predicted to sell 8 thousand units and a price of $2.50 is predicted to sell 12 thousand units. Using this model, a price of $3.00 is predicted to generate how many thousands in sales?

A. 10.75 thousand

B. 11.00 thousand

C. 11.25 thousand

D. 11.50 thousand

9. Patricia pays 17% income tax on every dollar she earns. She needs $1100 to buy a new refrigerator. How much does she need to earn so that she has $1100 after taxes?

A. $5981.38

B. $1794.41

C. $1325.30

D. None of the above

Gridded-Response: Fill in the grid with your answer to each question.

10. What is the growth factor of the equation $y = 14(0.98)^t$?

Extended-Response: Show your work for each question

11. Identify and explain the similarities between $y = 2^t$, and $y = (3 + t)^t$ when t gets large and small.

DATA ANALYSIS, STATISTICS, AND PROBABILITY

Displays of Data

A1,A2,A4 Construct and analyze circle graphs, bar graphs, histograms, box-and-whisker plots, scatter plots, and tables, and demonstrate the strengths and weaknesses of each format by choosing appropriately among them for a given situation. Use measures of central tendency and variability, such as, mean, median, maximum, minimum, range, standard deviation, quartile, and percentile, to describe, compare and draw conclusions about sets of data. Know the influence of outliers on various measures and representations of data about real-world and mathematical problems.

Select the best answer for each question.

Use the data table to answer questions 1–3.

Salary	Number of Employees
Under $50,000	45
$50,001–$60,000	55
$60,001–$70,000	77
$70,001–$80,000	52
$80,001–$90,000	90
Over $90,000	41

1. What is the best way to graphically represent the data?

   A. Box and whisker plot

   B. Scatter plot

   C. Line graph

   D. Histogram

2. What is the median salary for the employees?

   A. Under $50,000

   B. $50,001–$60,000

   C. $60,001–$70,000

   D. $70,001–$80,000

3. What percent of employees make over $70,000?

   A. 11.4%

   B. 49.2%

   C. 50.8%

   D. 12.5%

Use the data table below to answer questions 4 and 5.

Year	Average Rain Fall (in.)
1998	33.6
1999	42.5
2000	37.5
2001	31.4
2002	48.9
2003	50.1

4. Which type of graph would best represent these data?

   A. Circle graph

   B. Box and whisker plot

   C. Bar graph

   D. Line graph

MN Test Prep Grade 11

5. Which box and whisker plot correctly represents the data?

A.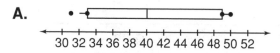

B.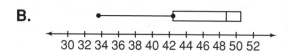

C.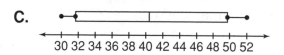

D.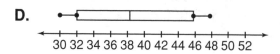

6. The table gives the median household income by race and ethnicity in 1999.

Race and Ethnicity	Median Household Income
Asian and Pacific Islander	$55,625
African American	$30,436
Hispanic	$33,455
White	$44,232

Which type of graph would best represent these data?

A. Circle graph

B. Histogram

C. Bar graph

D. Line graph

Gridded Response: Fill in the grid with your answer to each question.

7. Refer to the table.

Year	Average Cost for Electricity per Month	Average Cost for Natural Gas per Month
1998	$106	$21
1999	$86	$18
2000	$123	$29
2001	$135	$32
2002	$158	$51
2003	$146	$46

How many lines are included in a line graph of this data?

Extended Response: Show your work for each question.

8. The number of calls that 911 received during 18 randomly selected days are shown in the table.

51 71 81 41 91 42 52 61 72

43 62 31 63 64 82 53 44 65

A. Create a histogram for the number of calls.

B. Explain how you determined the range of each interval. Which interval had the greatest number of calls?

DATA ANALYSIS, STATISTICS, AND PROBABILITY

Measures of Data

A2,A1,A4 Use measures of central tendency and variability, such as, mean, median, maximum, minimum, range, standard deviation, quartile, and percentile, to describe, compare, and draw conclusions about sets of data. Construct and analyze circle graphs, bar graphs, histograms, box-and-whisker plots, scatter plots, and tables, and demonstrate the strengths and weaknesses of each format by choosing appropriately among them for a given situation. Know the influence of outliers on various measures and representations of data about real-world and mathematical problems.

Select the best answer for each question.

Use the box-and-whisker plots to answer questions 1–4.

Four different math groups took the same quiz. Their scores were plotted in the following box-and-whisker plots.

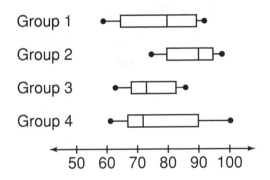

1. Which group had the lowest score?

   A. Group 1
   B. Group 2
   C. Group 3
   D. Group 4

2. Which group had the greatest range of scores?

   A. Group 1
   B. Group 2
   C. Group 3
   D. Group 4

3. Which group had the greatest Q_1 value?

   A. Group 1
   B. Group 2
   C. Group 3
   D. Group 4

4. Which group has the greatest median value?

   A. Group 1
   B. Group 2
   C. Group 3
   D. Group 4

5. What is the standard deviation for the following data set?

   4.1, 7.3, 4.8, 6.2, 5.1

   A. 1.13
   B. 1.15
   C. 1.26
   D. 1.52

MN Test Prep Grade 11

6. The mean of 13 yearly salaries is $512,542. Between which range of values would the sum of the salaries fall?

   A. $600,000–$650,000

   B. $6,000,000–$6,500,000

   C. $6,500,000–$6,750,000

   D. $6,750,000–$7,000,000

7. Which of the following sets of data contains 2 outliers?

   A. 33, 45, 10, 33, 29, 43, 39

   B. 51, 33, 66, 30, 44, 54, 44

   C. 15, 10, 22, 18, 11, 13, 19

   D. 40, 12, 46, 78, 33, 25, 30

Use the data set to answer questions 8–10.

   5.6, 7.2, 22.3, 8.2, 9.1, 8.2, 9.4, 6.3

8. What is the mean of the data?

   A. 8.2

   B. 8.478

   C. 9.305

   D. 9.5375

9. What effect does the outlier have on the mean of the given data?

   A. It raises the mean about 2 points.

   B. It raises the mean about 1.8 points

   C. It has no effect on the mean.

   D. It lowers the mean by 2 points.

10. Once the outlier is removed, what is the value of the range?

   A. 3.5

   B. 3.8

   C. 8.2

   D. 14.1

Gridded Response: Fill in the grid with your answer to each question.

11. Diego's test scores in his Advanced Placement English class are 95, 92, 98, 90, and 89.
He wants to achieve a semester average of 94. What scores must he receive on the next test?

Extended Response: Show your work for each question.

12. The following are the heights (in inches) of the players on the women's varsity basketball team.

   72 75 60 72 71 70 72 73 70 74

   A. What is the outlier in this data set? Explain why it is an outlier.

   B. What effect does removing this value have on the mean and the standard deviation?

Name_____ Date _____ Class_____

DATA ANALYSIS, STATISTICS, AND PROBABILITY

Experimental Probability

B6,B2,A7 Use a variety of experimental, simulation, and theoretical methods to calculate probabilities. Use area, trees, unions, and intersections to calculate probabilities and relate the results to mutual exclusiveness, independence, and conditional probabilities, in real-world and mathematical problems. Compare outcomes of voting methods such as majority, plurality, ranked by preference, run-off, and pair-wise comparison.

Select the best answer for each question.

Use the information to answer questions 1–3.

You spin a spinner with 6 colors: red, yellow, pink, green, blue, and white. You record your results in the table.

Outcome	Frequency
Red	8
Yellow	3
Pink	9
Green	7
Blue	5
White	8

1. What is the experimental probability that the spinner will land on blue on the next spin?

   A. $\frac{1}{5}$ C. $\frac{3}{40}$

   B. $\frac{1}{8}$ D. $\frac{7}{40}$

2. What is the experimental probability that the spinner will NOT land on red on the next spin?

   A. $\frac{1}{10}$ C. $\frac{3}{5}$

   B. $\frac{1}{5}$ D. $\frac{4}{5}$

3. Which of the following is true about the table?

   A. The experimental probability that the spinner will land on red next is equal to the probability that the spinner will land on yellow next.

   B. The experimental probability that the spinner will land on red or yellow next is equal to the probability that the spinner will land on pink next.

   C. The probability that the spinner will land on red next is equal to the probability that the spinner will land on white next.

   D. The experimental probability that the spinner will land on green next is the smallest probability.

MN Test Prep Grade 11

Use the information to answer questions 4–6.

Bright Light Bulbs produces 1400 light bulbs in one day. Of those, 7 light bulbs were found to be defective.

4. What is the experimental probability that a light bulb produced that day was defective?

   A. 0.002

   B. 0.003

   C. 0.004

   D. 0.005

5. What is the experimental probability that a light bulb produced that day was NOT defective?

   A. 0.995

   B. 0.996

   C. 0.997

   D. 0.998

6. A newspaper reporter claimed that one-third of all sushi contains dangerous toxins. If the newest sushi bar in the city serves 1500 pieces of sushi each day, how many pieces are reportedly dangerous?

   A. 100

   B. 250

   C. 300

   D. 500

Gridded Response: Fill in the grid with your answer to each question.

7. Predict approximately how many light bulbs will be defective when 2600 light bulbs are produced the following week.

Extended Response: Show your work for each question.

8. A. Design an experiment with a 10-sided die. The experiment should have the following types of outcomes:

   • Highly probable

   • Equally probable

   • Improbable

   • Impossible

   B. Explain how you would test your experiment.

MN Test Prep Grade 11

DATA ANALYSIS, STATISTICS, AND PROBABILITY

Surveys and Samples

B5,A6,A4 Know the effect of sample size on experimental and simulation probabilities. Interpret data credibility in the context of measurement error and display distortion. Know the influence of outliers on various measures and representations of data about real-world and mathematical problems.

Select the best answer for each question.

1. To find whether Greek salad should be offered in the school cafeteria, the student council wants to try one of the following methods:

   I   They will ask members of the school marching band.

   II They will ask the teachers.

   III They will ask 10 randomly selected students from each grade.

   Which methods are biased?

   A. All are biased
   B. None are biased
   C. I and II
   D. II and III

2. Consider these two survey questions:

   I   Which would you prefer for lunch: a pizza, a hamburger, or fried chicken?

   II Would you prefer fried chicken for lunch to a boring pizza or hamburger?

   Which is biased?

   A. I is biased.
   B. II is biased.
   C. Both are biased.
   D. Neither are biased.

3. There are 60 students in the eleventh grade.

   Which of the ways below are methods to produce a random sample of eleventh-grade students?

   A. Put all the names of students in a hat, then choose names for the sample.
   B. Input the names into a computer. Then, use software to generate names randomly.
   C. All of the above are methods to produce a random sample.
   D. None of the above are methods to produce a random sample.

4. Tom wants to find the least-liked cafeteria food.

Which method describes a self-selected sample?

A. Tom randomly chooses 100 students and asks them which cafeteria food they like least.

B. Tom asks every 10th student that walks in the school's front door in the morning which cafeteria food they like least.

C. Tom posts a sign on the cafeteria door, asking students to check off which food they like least.

D. All of the above describe self-selected samples.

Use the situation described for questions 5–6.

A clothing manufacturer tests every 50th pair of jeans for quality control.

5. What is the population?

A. Every 50th pair of jeans

B. The quality testers at the clothing manufacturer

C. All the jeans made by the clothing manufacturer

D. All the workers at the clothing manufacturer

6. What is the sample?

A. Every 50th pair of jeans

B. The quality testers at the clothing manufacturer

C. All the jeans made by the clothing manufacturer

D. All the workers at the clothing manufacturer

Gridded Response: Fill in the grid with your answer to each question.

7. There are 1000 students at Tech High School. How many students should be sampled to find what transportation students use to get to school?

Extended Response: Show your work for each question.

8. Identify the method of sampling used.

A. Erica wanted to find the favorite flower of the teachers at her school. She puts up a sign in the staff room asking teachers to check off their favorite flower.

B. Liam wants to find out what theme the next school dance should be. He randomly selects 25 students from each grade and surveys them.

9. Identify the population in the situation. The management team at a shopping mall in Albuquerque wants to know how to attract more people between the ages of 18–35 to the mall.

Name_____ Date _____ Class_____

DATA ANALYSIS, STATISTICS, AND PROBABILITY

Theoretical Probability

B4,B3,B2 For simple probability models, determine the expected values of random variables. Use area, trees, unions, and intersections to calculate probabilities and relate the results to mutual exclusiveness, independence, and conditional probabilities, in real-world and mathematical problems. Use probability models, including area and binomial models, in real-world and mathematical problems.

Select the best answer for each question.

Use the information to answer questions 1 and 2.

The odds are 1:4 that it will rain tomorrow.

1. What is the probability that it will rain tomorrow?
   A. $\frac{1}{3}$ C. $\frac{1}{4}$
   B. $\frac{1}{5}$ D. $\frac{3}{4}$

2. What is the probability that it will not rain tomorrow?
   A. $\frac{3}{4}$ C. $\frac{2}{5}$
   B. $\frac{4}{5}$ D. $\frac{1}{5}$

Use the information to answer questions 3 and 4.

Box 1 contains 5 red marbles and 5 blue marbles. Box 2 contains 6 red marbles and 2 blue marbles.

3. If you chose a marble from each box, what is the probability that both marbles are blue?
   A. 10%   C. 16.6%
   B. 12.5%   D. 20%

4. If you pick a marble from Box 1 and from Box 2, what is the probability that the first marble will be blue and the second marble will be red?
   A. $\frac{1}{8}$
   B. $\frac{3}{8}$
   C. $\frac{5}{8}$
   D. $\frac{7}{8}$

Use the information to answer questions 5 and 6.

A number cube has 6 sides with the numbers 1 to 6. It is rolled twice.

5. Which event has a probability of 75%?
   A. Rolling a number divisible by 2 at least once
   B. Rolling a sum of less than 7
   C. Rolling a number greater than 3
   D. Rolling two even numbers

6. Which situation has a probability of $\frac{1}{6}$?
   A. Rolling a sum of 7
   B. Rolling an odd number or a 2
   C. Rolling a multiple of 4 or rolling a 3
   D. Rolling a multiple of 3

MN Test Prep Grade 11

Name_____ Date _____ Class_____

Use the information to answer questions 7 and 8.

Ten cards are numbered from 1 to 10. A card is selected at random and replaced. A second card is randomly selected and replaced. A third card is randomly selected. All selections are recorded.

7. What is the probability of selecting three even-numbered cards?

   A. $\dfrac{1}{2}$

   B. $\dfrac{1}{3}$

   C. $\dfrac{1}{4}$

   D. $\dfrac{1}{8}$

8. What is the probability of drawing 3 cards that are multiples of 5?

   A. $\dfrac{1}{5}$

   B. $\dfrac{1}{25}$

   C. $\dfrac{1}{50}$

   D. $\dfrac{1}{125}$

Gridded Response: Fill in the grid with your answer to each question.

9. A fair coin with a head and a tail is tossed 3 times. What is the probability that no heads come up? Give your answer in the form of a percentage.

Extended Response: Show your work for each question.

10. The table below shows all the possible outcomes of rolling two number cubes.

(1,1)	(1,2)	(1,3)	(1,4)	(1,5)	(1,6)
(2,1)	(2,2)	(2,3)	(2,4)	(2,5)	(2,6)
(3,1)	(3,2)	(3,3)	(3,4)	(3,5)	(3,6)
(4,1)	(4,2)	(4,3)	(4,4)	(4,5)	(4,6)
(5,1)	(5,2)	(5,3)	(5,4)	(5,5)	(5,6)
(6,1)	(6,2)	(6,3)	(6,4)	(6,5)	(6,6)

   A. What is the probability of rolling a sum of 2 or a sum of 8?

   B. What is the probability of rolling a sum greater than 6?

DATA ANALYSIS, STATISTICS, AND PROBABILITY

Dependent and Independent Events

A5,B2,B3,A7 Understand the relationship between correlation and causation. Use area, trees, unions, and intersections to calculate probabilities and relate the results to mutual exclusiveness, independence, and conditional probabilities, in real-world and mathematical problems. Use probability models, including area and binomial models, in real-world and mathematical problems. Compare outcomes of voting methods such as majority, plurality, ranked by preference, run-off, and pair-wise comparison.

1. If the probability of a pitcher throwing a strike is $\frac{2}{5}$, what is the probability that he will throw three consecutive strikes?

A. $\frac{4}{25}$

B. $\frac{8}{25}$

C. $\frac{4}{125}$

D. $\frac{8}{125}$

2. If Team A has a $\frac{1}{20}$ chance of winning the basketball championship and Team B has a $\frac{1}{10}$ chance, what is the chance that Team A or B will win?

A. $\frac{3}{20}$

B. $\frac{3}{10}$

C. $\frac{1}{15}$

D. $\frac{1}{200}$

3. There is a bag of marbles with 4 blue marbles and 8 green marbles. If Jason pulls out 6 green marbles, then puts them back in the back, what is the probability that the next one will be green?

A. $\frac{2}{3}$

B. $\frac{1}{3}$

C. $\frac{1}{2}$

D. $\frac{3}{4}$

4. Referring to question 3, if Jason did not replace the original 6 marbles, then what is the probability that the next one will be green?

A. $\frac{2}{3}$

B. $\frac{1}{3}$

C. $\frac{1}{2}$

D. $\frac{3}{4}$

MN Test Prep Grade 11

5. If there is a 20% chance Johan will go to the baseball game and a 30% chance that Roger will go to the game, what is the chance that they both will be at the game?

   A. 60%

   B. 50%

   C. 6%

   D. None of the above

6. If the probability that a student will get an A on a test is 0.25, what is the probability that he or she will get two consecutive A's?

   A. $\frac{1}{2}$

   B. $\frac{1}{4}$

   C. $\frac{1}{16}$

   D. $\frac{1}{25}$

7. Referring to question 6, would the answer change if you knew that a different student got an A on the last two tests?

   A. Yes

   B. No

   C. It might

   D. Not enough information

Use the following information to answer questions 8 and 9.

There is a 20% chance of rain on Monday and a 30% chance of rain on Tuesday.

8. What is the probability that the next two days will have no rain?

   A. 16%   C. 44%

   B. 28%   D. 56%

9. What is the probability that it will rain both days?

   A. 6%   C. 22%

   B. 14%   D. 28%

10. The school is having a draw to win a digital camera. If 20 boys and 30 girls entered, what is the probability that a girl will win?

   A. $\frac{2}{3}$ C. $\frac{3}{5}$

   B. $\frac{3}{2}$ D. $\frac{2}{5}$

11. If a different draw was being held, with 20 boys and 20 girls, what is the probability that both winners will be girls?

   A. $\frac{1}{2}$ C. $\frac{7}{10}$

   B. $\frac{11}{10}$ D. $\frac{3}{10}$

Gridded Response: Fill in the grid with your answer to each question.

12. If Chris rolls two dice, what is the probability that he will roll two ones? Round your answer to the nearest percent.

Extended Response: Show your work for each question.

13. Referring to questions 10 and 11, If a third draw was held, with 16 boys and 24 girls, what is the probability that a boy will win the third draw?

DATA ANALYSIS, STATISTICS, AND PROBABILITY

Scatter Plots

A3,A1,A4 Determine an approximate best-fit line from a given scatter plot and use the line to draw conclusions. Select and apply appropriate counting procedures to solve real-world and mathematical problems, including probability problems. Know the influence of outliers on various measures and representations of data about real-world and mathematical problems.

Select the best answer for each question.

1. Which scatter plot shows a positive correlation between two variables for a set of data?

A. 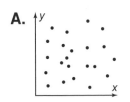   C.

B. 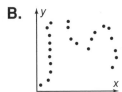   D.

Use the graph to answer questions 2 and 3.

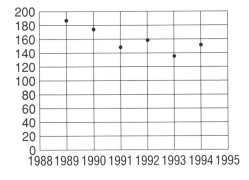

2. Which is true of the value of the slope of the line of best fit?

A. The slope of the line of best fit is positive.

B. The slope of the line of best fit is negative.

C. The slope of the line of best fit is zero.

D. None of the above.

3. Suppose the trend in enrollment continues. Predict the enrollment in 1995.

A. 110

B. 130

C. 150

D. 170

MN Test Prep Grade 11

Name_____ Date _____ Class_____

Use these figures to answer questions 4–6.

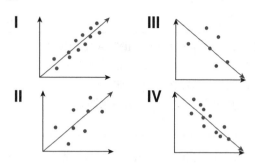

4. Which graphs show a positive correlation?

A. Graphs I and II

B. Graphs III and IV

C. Graphs I and IV

D. It is impossible to tell without labels on the graphs.

5. Which graphs show a negative correlation?

A. Graphs I and II

B. Graphs III and IV

C. Graphs I and IV

D. It is impossible to tell without labels on the graphs.

6. Which graphs show a strong correlation?

A. Graphs I and II

B. Graphs III and IV

C. Graphs I and IV

D. Graphs II and III

Gridded Response: Fill in the grid with your answer to each question.

7. Using the graph from question 2, how many students enrolled in 1992?

Extended Response: Show your work for each question.

8. The graph shows the relationship between car ownership and household income.

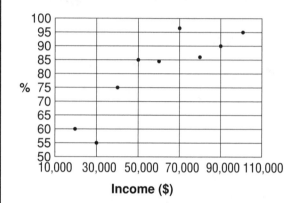

A. Explain any trends in the data.

B. Suppose a household had an income of $150,000. How likely would they be to own a car? Explain.

MN Test Prep Grade 11

DATA ANALYSIS, STATISTICS, AND PROBABILITY

Counting

A7,B6,B3 Compare outcomes of voting methods such as majority, plurality, ranked by preference, run-off, and pair-wise comparison. Use a variety of experimental, simulation and theoretical methods to calculate probabilities. Use probability models, including area and binomial models, in real-world and mathematical problems.

Select the best answer for each question.

1. Cara has 8 CDs in her collection. She wants to put 5 CDs in her CD player. How many different ways can she put CDs into her player?

   A. 5   **C.** 1680

   B. 40   **D.** 6720

2. How many different ways can 6 people be seated around a 72-inch round table?

   A. 6   **C.** 30

   B. 12   **D.** 720

3. How many outcomes are possible if you spin the spinner shown below four times to make a four-digit number?

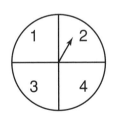

   A. 8

   B. 16

   C. 64

   D. 256

4. Ling is putting together a menu for different box lunches. Customers can chose from 4 types of lunch meats, 3 types of cheese, 4 types of chips, 3 types of fruit, and 4 types of drinks. Which expression best describes the number of different box lunches that are possible?

   A. $4 + 4 + 4 + 3 + 3$

   B. $4^3 + 3^2$

   C. 4×3

   D. $3 \times 3 \times 4 \times 4 \times 4$

5. John is designing his own vanity license plate for his car. He must use 2 letters and 3 numbers. The numbers and letters in the vanity plate may NOT be repeated and must take the form of letter, letter, number, number, number. How many different choices are possible for John's vanity plate?

   A. 1560   **C.** 468,000

   B. 52,000   **D.** 650,000

6. Two swimming teams line up for practice. If there are 6 swimmers on Team A and 8 swimmers on Team B, how many more different lineup combinations does Team B have than Team A?

   A. 14   **C.** 39,600

   B. 48   **D.** 40,320

7. The Latin Club is choosing its officers for the next school year. They must choose a president, a vice president, a secretary, a treasurer, and a historian from its 25 members. How many ways can the club choose its officers?

   A. $_{25}P_5$
   B. $_5C_{20}$
   C. $_{25}C_5$
   D. $_5P_{20}$

8. Which of the following has the smallest number of possible outcomes?

   A. Tossing a number cube 3 times
   B. Selecting a team of 3 people from a group of 8 people
   C. Choosing one fruit and one vegetable from 2 fruits and 3 vegetables
   D. Selecting 4 books to buy from a group of 20 books

9. Which table represents the values of $_8P_r$ for the given values of r?

   A.

r	$_8P_r$
3	336
4	1680
5	6720

   B.

r	$_8P_r$
3	24
4	32
5	40

   C.

r	$_8P_r$
3	512
4	4096
5	32,768

   D.

r	$_8P_r$
3	11
4	12
5	13

Gridded Response: Fill in the grid with your answer to each question.

10. Brady is choosing which vegetables to plant in his last three sections of his garden. He must choose three different vegetables of the following types: carrots, green beans, potatoes, broccoli, tomatoes, and corn. How many different groups of vegetables can he plant?

Extended Response: Show your work for each question.

11. Lexie can choose several options for her new car. There are 9 exterior colors, 3 interior colors, 5 stereo systems, and 6 types of fabric. In how many ways can Lexie choose one of each category?

MN Test Prep Grade 11

SPATIAL SENSE, GEOMETRY, AND MEASUREMENT

Three-dimensional figures (nets)

A1 Use models and visualization to understand and represent three-dimensional objects and their cross sections from different perspectives.

Select the best answer for each question.

1. Which figure is a net for a octahedron?

A.

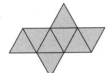

B.

C.

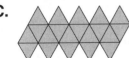

D.

2. A solid has 4 congruent triangular faces. What is the solid?

   A. triangular prism

   B. rectangular prism

   C. triangular pyramid

   D. rectangular pyramid

3. This figure is the net for an object. What is the object?

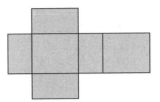

   A. triangular pyramid

   B. rectangular pyramid

   C. triangular prism

   D. rectangular prism

4. Which are the faces of an heptagonal pyramid?

   A. 7 triangular faces and 1 heptagonal face

   B. 1 octagonal face and 8 rectangular faces

   C. 7 rectangular faces and 2 heptagonal faces

   D. 10 rectangular faces

5. Which solid has 2 congruent hexagonal faces and 6 congruent rectangular faces?

   A. hexagonal pyramid

   B. hexagonal prism

   C. rectangular pyramid

   D. rectangular prism

     MN Test Prep Grade 11

6. Which object is represented in these views?

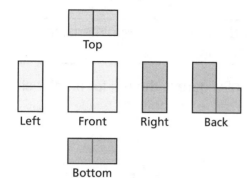

Top

 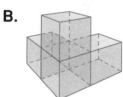

Left   Front   Right   Back

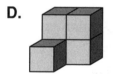

Bottom

A.

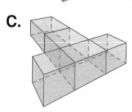

B.

C.

D.

7. Which in NOT an orthographic view of this object?

A.

B.

C.

D.

Gridded Response: Fill in the grid with your answer to each question.

8. How many vertices does a cone have?

Extended Response: Show your work for each question.

9. Describe or draw two figures that have the same left, right, front, and back orthographic views but have different top and bottom views.

MN Test Prep Grade 11

SPATIAL SENSE, GEOMETRY, AND MEASUREMENT

Triangles

B1 Know and use theorems about triangles and parallel lines in elementary geometry to justify facts about various geometrical figures and solve real-world and mathematical problems. These theorems include criteria for two triangles to be congruent or similar and facts about parallel lines cut by a transversal.

1. The two rectangles are similar. What is the unknown length? Round your answer to the nearest hundredth.

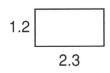 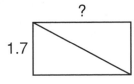

A. 1.42   **C.** 2.68

B. 1.62   **D.** 3.26

2. The triangles below are similar. What is the perimeter of the larger triangle?

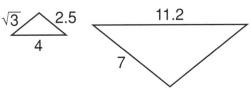

A. 8.23   **C.** 25.2

B. 18.82   **D.** 23.05

3. The right triangles drawn below are similar. What is the approximate value of x?

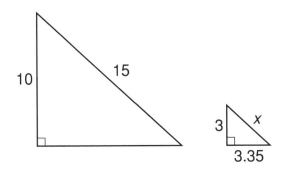

A. 5   **C.** 4

B. 4.5   **D.** 3.5

4. The height and base of the large right triangle shown measure 25 feet and 38 feet respectively. If a horizontal plank extends from the hypotenuse to the shorter leg 12 feet above the base, how long is it?

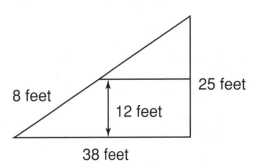

A. 4.16 feet   **C.** 13 feet

B. 6.24 feet   **D.** 19.76 feet

5. What value of x results in two similar right triangles?

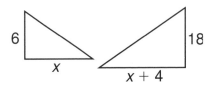

A. $x = 1$

B. $x = 2$

C. $x = 3$

D. $x = 4$

6. For parallelograms *ABCD* and *QRST* to be similar, which of the following must be true?

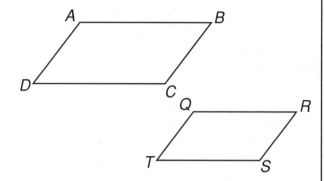

A. The four angles in ▱*ABCD* have to be congruent to the four angles in ▱*QRST*.

B. The four sides in ▱*ABCD* have to be congruent to the four sides in ▱*QRST*.

C. At least two of the adjacent sides in ▱*ABCD* have to be congruent to two of the adjacent sides in ▱*QRST*.

D. The angles in ▱*ABCD* have to be congruent to the corresponding angles in ▱*QRST*.

7. A designer wants the ratio of the two adjacent sides of a rectangular frame to be 16:11. If the longest side of the frame is 32 inches, how long is the diagonal of the frame?

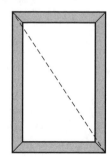

A. 11 in. **C.** 32 in.

B. 16 in. **D.** 39 in.

Gridded Response: Fill in the grid with your answer to each question.

8. Triangles *ABC* and *XYZ* are similar and the length of $\overline{AB}$ is 9 cm, the length of $\overline{BC}$ is 34 cm, the length of $\overline{AC}$ is 14 cm and the length of $\overline{YZ}$ is 68 cm. What is the length of $\overline{XY}$ in centimeters?

9. Triangles *ABC* and *XYZ* are similar and m∠*A* = 34° and m∠*Y* = 62°. What is the measure, in degrees, of angle *C*?

Extended Response: Show your work for each question.

10. List all the theorems you can use to prove that two triangles are similar.

MN Test Prep Grade 11

SPATIAL SENSE, GEOMETRY, AND MEASUREMENT

Parallel Lines/Angles

> B1,B5 Know and use theorems about triangles and parallel lines in elementary geom-
> etry to justify facts about various geometrical figures and solve real-world and mathe-
> matical problems. These theorems include criteria for two triangles to be congruent or
> similar and facts about parallel lines cut by a transversal.Use coordinate geometry to
> represent and examine geometric concepts such as the distance between two points,
> the midpoint of a line segment, the slope of a line, and the slopes of parallel and per-
> pendicular lines.

Select the best answer for each question.

1. Find y.

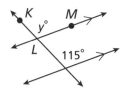

    A. 75   **C.** 144

    B. 115   **D.** 178

2. For 2 parallel lines and a transversal, $m\angle 1 = 83°$. For which pair of angle measures is the sum the least?

    A. $\angle 1$ and a corresponding angle

    B. $\angle 1$ and a same-side interior angle

    C. $\angle 1$ and its supplement

    D. $\angle 1$ and its complement

3. Two coplanar lines are cut by a transversal. Which condition does NOT guarantee that the two lines are parallel?

    A. A pair of alternate interior angles are congruent.

    B. A pair of alternate exterior angles are complementary.

    C. A pair of same-side interior angles are supplementary.

    D. A pair of corresponding angles are congruent.

Use the following figure to answer questions 4–6.

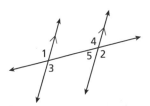

4. If $m\angle 1 = 120°$ and $m\angle 2 = (60x)°$, what is the value of x?

    A. 1   **C.** 5

    B. 2   **D.** 10

5. If $m\angle 3 = (50x + 20)°$ and $m\angle 4 = (100x - 80)°$, what is $m\angle 3$?

    A. 60

    B. 90

    C. 120

    D. 180

6. Which postulate or theorem is best-suited for finding the answer to #5?

    A. Alternate Exterior Angles Theorem

    B. Corresponding Angles Postulate

    C. Same-Side Interior Angles Theorem

    D. Alternate Interior Angles Theorem

Name_____ Date _____ Class_____

7. Find the value of x so that ℓ ∥ m.

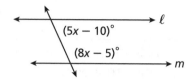

(5x − 10)°
(8x − 5)°

A. 5   **C.** 15
B. 12   **D.** 33

8. Find the complement of ∠F.

59°
F

A. 11°   **C.** 51°
B. 31°   **D.** 121°

Gridded Response: Fill in the grid with your answer to each question.

9. Use this figure for parts A and B.

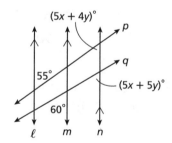

(5x + 4y)°
p
q
55°
(5x + 5y)°
60°
ℓ   m   n

A. Find y.
B. Find x.

10. Use this figure for parts A and B.

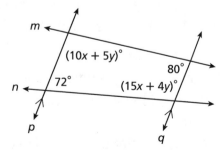

m
(10x + 5y)°
80°
n
72°
(15x + 4y)°
p
q

A. Find x.
B. Find y.

Extended Response: Show your work for each question.

11. Given: m∠SRT = 25° and m∠SUR = 65°

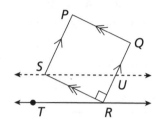

P
Q
S
U
T   R

A. Name a same-side interior angle of ∠SUR for lines SU and RT with transversal $\overline{RU}$.
B. Prove that $\overleftrightarrow{SU} \parallel \overleftrightarrow{RT}$.

SPATIAL SENSE, GEOMETRY, AND MEASUREMENT

Circles

B2 Know and use theorems about circles to justify geometrical facts and solve real-world and mathematical problems. These theorems include the relationships involving tangent lines and radii, the relationship between inscribed and central angles and the relationship between the measure of a central angle and arc length.

Select the best answer for each question. Use 3.14 for π.

1. Justin's bicycle tire is 26 inches in diameter. What is the circumference of the tire?

   A. 26 inches

   B. 91.4 inches

   C. 81.64 inches

   D. 18.84 inches

2. In the figure, $\overline{AX} = 0.26$, $\overline{XC} = 0.91$, and $\overline{DX} = 0.27$, find $\overline{XB}$.

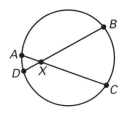

   A. 0.88

   B. 0.945

   C. 1.01

   D. 1.13

Use this figure for questions 3 and 4.

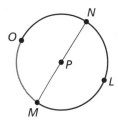

3. Which is a minor arc of circle *P*?

   A. $\overparen{MO}$

   B. $\overparen{MLO}$

   C. $\overparen{MN}$

   D. $\overparen{ONL}$

4. Which is a major arc of circle *P*?

   A. $\overparen{MO}$

   B. $\overparen{MLO}$

   C. $\overparen{MN}$

   D. $\overparen{ONL}$

5. A 10-foot circular garden is to be filled in with sod. How many square feet of sod are required to fill in the garden?

   A. About 79 square feet

   B. About 85 square feet

   C. About 90 square feet

   D. About 94 square feet

Name_____ Date _____ Class_____

Use this figure for questions 6 to 8.

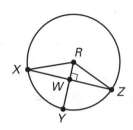

$\overline{RY} \perp \overline{XZ}$ at W

6. Fill in the blank: $\overline{XW} \cong$ _____

   A. $\overline{RW}$

   B. $\overline{WY}$

   C. $\overline{RY}$

   D. $\overline{WZ}$

7. If $RY = 7$ and $RW = 2$, what is XW to the nearest tenth?

   A. 4.3

   B. 5.9

   C. 6.7

   D. 7.4

8. If $RY = 3$ and $RW = 2$, what is WZ to the nearest tenth?

   A. 1.4

   B. 1.8

   C. 2.2

   D. 2.9

Gridded Response: Fill in the grid with your answer to each question.

9. The center of a circle is $C(0, 2)$, and the endpoint of one of its radii is $W(-6, -4)$. If $\overline{WZ}$ is a diameter of the circle, what is the x-coordinate of Z?

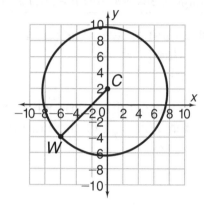

Extended Response: Show your work for each question.

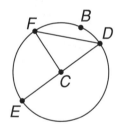

10. A. What is the angle measure of $\angle CDF$ if $\overline{FC}$ bisects $\angle ECD$?

   B. List two major arcs and two minor arcs for the circle.

   C. If $EC = 3$ cm, what is the length of $\overline{FD}$?

   D. What is $\overline{DB}$ called? Also if $m\angle DCB = 30°$, what is the angle measure of $\angle ECB$?

Name_____ Date _____ Class_____

SPATIAL SENSE, GEOMETRY, AND MEASUREMENT

Perimeter, Area and Circumference

B3 Know and use properties of two- and three-dimensional figures to solve real-world and mathematical problems such as: finding area, perimeter, volume, and surface area; applying direct or indirect methods of measurement; the Pythagorean theorem and its converse; and properties of 45°-45°-90° and 30°-60°-90° triangles.

Select the best answer for each question.

Use the information to answer questions 1 and 2.

A designer plans to create a garden around the town's oldest tree. He wants to center a square around the tree to protect it. Each side of the square will be 26 feet long. The garden will be a circle centered around the square. The area of the garden should be 33,286 square feet, not including the area of the square.

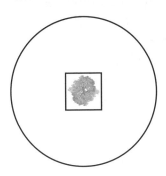

1. What should the radius of the circle be? Use $\pi = 3.14$.

   A. 95 feet

   B. 100 feet

   C. 102 feet

   D. 104 feet

2. The designer is planning to put a brick walkway around the edge of the circular garden. How long should the walkway be?

   A. 60 feet

   B. 600 feet

   C. 653 feet

   D. 682 feet

Use the information to answer questions 3–5.

A bicycle path forms a rectangle with a perimeter of 18 miles. The area surrounded by the bicycle path is 20 square miles.

3. Which system of equations can be used to solve for the length and width of the bicycle path?

   A. $2x + 2y = 20$
   $xy = 18$

   B. $x + y = 20$
   $xy = 18$

   C. $2x + 2y = 18$
   $xy = 20$

   D. $2x + y = 20$
   $xy = 18$

MN Test Prep Grade 11

4. What is the width of the rectangle formed by the bicycle path?

    A. 4 miles

    B. 1 mile

    C. 7 miles

    D. 10 miles

5. A boy bicycles the path 2.5 times. How many miles did he ride?

    A. 30 miles

    B. 40 miles

    C. 45 miles

    D. 60 miles

6. A regular pentagon has sides 4.8 m long. If the side lengths are reduced by 30%, what is the perimeter of the new pentagon?

    A. 7.2 m

    B. 16.8 m

    C. 24 m

    D. 31.2 m

Gridded Response: Fill in the grid with your answer to each question.

7. The perimeter of a square hospital room is 34 yards. How many yards do each side of the room measure?

Extended Response: Show your work for each question.

8. The following diagram shows a house and the land surrounding the house. The dimensions of the house are given in feet. The lot is a circle of radius 80 feet.

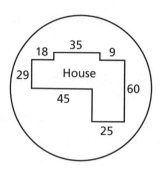

    A. A landscaper plans to plant tulip bulbs around the perimeter of the house. Find the perimeter of the house and then determine how many tulip bulbs he needs if he plans to plant 2 tulip bulbs per linear foot.

    B. The interior lighting designer needs to know the area of the interior of the house. Find the area of the house. Then determine how much the designer will charge for her consulting fee if she charges $2.50 per square foot.

    C. The landscaper has to spread fertilizer in the entire yard. A bag of fertilizer covers 2000 square feet. How many full bags of fertilizer does he need to buy? If the cost of fertilizer is $6.99 per bag, how much does the fertilizer cost?

SPATIAL SENSE, GEOMETRY, AND MEASUREMENT

Indirect Measurement

B3,B6 Know and use properties of two- and three-dimensional figures to solve real-world and mathematical problems such as: finding area, perimeter, volume, and surface area; applying direct or indirect methods of measurement; the Pythagorean theorem and its converse; and properties of 45°-45°-90° and 30°-60°-90° triangles. Use numeric, graphic, and symbolic representations of transformations such as reflections, translations and change of scale in one, two, and three dimensions to solve real-world and mathematical problems.

Select the best answer for each question.

Use the following information to answer questions 1 and 2.

Suppose $\triangle ABC \cong \triangle XYZ$ and $\overline{AB} = 1.2$, $\overline{BC} = 1.0$, $\overline{AC} = 5.8$, and $\overline{XY} = 5.8$

1. What is the length of $\overline{YZ}$?

   A. 6.2

   B. 1.0

   C. 5.8

   D. 1.2

2. What is the length of $\overline{XZ}$?

   A. 1.0

   B. 6.2

   C. 5.8

   D. 1.2

3. A landscape architect sets up the congruent triangles shown in the figure to find the distance JK across a pond. The perimeter of $\triangle LMN$ is 172 ft. What is JK?

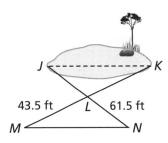

   A. 31 ft

   B. 117 ft

   C. 67 ft

   D. 35 ft

4. Given that $\triangle DEF \cong \triangle JKL$, x equals which of the following values?

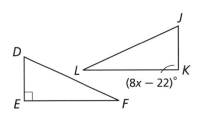

   A. 14

   B. 90

   C. 104

   D. 88

Name_____ Date _____ Class_____

5. Given $\triangle PQR \cong \triangle XYZ$, which of the following are congruent corresponding parts to $\overline{PQ}$ and $\angle X$?

   A. $\overline{YZ}$ and $\angle R$

   B. $\overline{YZ}$ and $\angle P$

   C. $\overline{XY}$ and $\angle P$

   D. $\overline{YZ}$ and $\angle Q$

6. If $\triangle ABC \cong \triangle CDA$ as shown in the figure, what is the value of y and of AB?

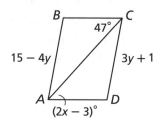

   A. 25 and 2

   B. 2 and 7

   C. 22 and 2

   D. 25 and 7

Use this figure for questions 7 and 8.

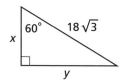

For each question, express your answer in simplest radical form.

7. Find the value of x.

   A. $2\sqrt{7}$

   B. 72

   C. $3\sqrt{9}$

   D. $9\sqrt{3}$

8. Find the value of y.

   A. $2\sqrt{27}$

   B. 72

   C. $3\sqrt{9}$

   D. 27

Gridded Response: Fill in the grid with your answer to each question.

9. A 30°-60°-90° triangle's shorter leg is 5 cm. Find the length of the hypotenuse in centimeters.

10. A 45°-45°-90° triangle has a leg that is 7 cm. Find the length of the hypotenuse to the nearest centimeter.

Extended Response: Show your work for each question.

11. A 30°-60°-90° triangle's shorter leg is 15 cm. Find the approximate length of the longer leg.

12. If the sides of a special right triangle are 3 and $3\sqrt{3}$, what is the length of the hypotenuse? Will the value of cos 60° change if the sides were to change in a special right triangle?

Name_____ Date _____ Class_____

SPATIAL SENSE, GEOMETRY, AND MEASUREMENT

Surface Area and Volume

B3 Know and use properties of two- and three-dimensional figures to solve real-world and mathematical problems such as: finding area, perimeter, volume, and surface area; applying direct or indirect methods of measurement; the Pythagorean theorem and its converse; and properties of 45°-45°-90° and 30°-60°-90° triangles.

Select the best answer for each question.

1. Determine the volume of a hemisphere with radius 10.5 ft. Round your answer to the nearest hundredth if necessary.

   A. 4849.05 ft^3

   B. 2424.52 ft^3

   C. 1212.26 ft^3

   D. 2424.50 ft^3

Use this figure for questions 2 and 9.

The gift box has a volume of 4972.8 cubic inches.

2. Determine the height, *h*, of the figure.

   A. 21.2 in.

   B. 23.5 in

   C. 22.2 in.

   D. 24.0 in.

3. A hostess wants to cut a wedge of cheese that has a volume of 180 cubic inches. What should the width, *w*, be?

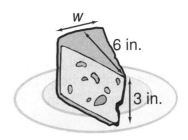

   A. 18 in.   C. 20 in.

   B. 19 in.   D. 21 in.

4. One quart of liquid corresponds to a volume of 57.75 cubic inches. What is the volume of 1 gallon of liquid?

   A. 113 cubic inches

   B. 200 cubic inches

   C. 220 cubic inches

   D. 231 cubic inches

5. The rectangular base of Pyramid Arena in Memphis, Tennessee, covers 360,000 square feet. If the height is 321 feet, what is the volume of Pyramid Arena?

   A. 12,500,000 cubic feet

   B. 23,650,000 cubic feet

   C. 38,520,000 cubic feet

   D. 55,400,000 cubic feet

MN Test Prep Grade 11

Name_____ Date _____ Class_____

Use the figure shown below for questions 7 and 8.

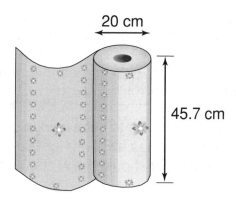

20 cm

45.7 cm

6. Determine the lateral area of a roll of paper towels with a height of 45.7 cm and a diameter of 20 cm.

   A. 1425.56 cm^2
   B. 2869.96 cm^2
   C. 3497.96 cm^2
   D. 4021.23 cm^2

7. Determine the volume of the roll of paper towels.

   A. 14,357.1 cm^3
   B. 14,349.8 cm^3
   C. 21,223.1 cm^3
   D. 24,357.1 cm^3

8. Determine the volume of a cone with a height of 14.2 mm and a radius of 5 cm (Use $\pi = 3.14$).

   A. 37.16 mm^3
   B. 37.16 cm^3
   C. 37.61 mm^3
   D. 37.61 cm^3

Gridded Response: Fill in the grid with your answer to each question.

9. Determine the surface area of the figure from question 2 in square inches.

Extended Response: Show your work for each question.

10. The Acme Water Specialists, Inc. manufactures cylindrical water tanks. A water tank has a height of 30 feet and a diameter of 15 feet. If possible, how many of these cylindrical tanks full of water could be poured into the Great Pyramid in Giza, given that the Pyramid has a height of 450 feet and a square base with area of 756 feet?

MN Test Prep Grade 11

Name_____ Date _____ Class_____

SPATIAL SENSE, GEOMETRY, AND MEASUREMENT

Pythagorean Theorem

B3 Know and use properties of two- and three-dimensional figures to solve real-world and mathematical problems such as: finding area, perimeter, volume, and surface area; applying direct or indirect methods of measurement; the Pythagorean theorem and its converse; and properties of 45°-45°-90° and 30°-60°-90° triangles.

Select the best answer for each question.

1. In the right triangle shown, what is the length of the unknown side?

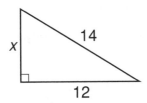

A. $\sqrt{26}$ C. $\sqrt{52}$

B. 26   D. $\sqrt{340}$

2. The circle has a radius of 12 units. A triangle is formed by connecting a point on the perimeter of the circle with the endpoints of the diameter. What is the perimeter of the triangle? Write your answer in simplest radical form.

A. $24\left(1 + \sqrt{2}\,\right)$ units

B. $48\sqrt{2}$ units

C. $24 + \sqrt{2}$ units

D. $24 + \sqrt{288}$ units

3. A hiker hikes due west from camp and then due south. He hikes 16 fewer miles due south than twice the number of miles he hikes due west. If the hiker is 40 miles from camp, how far did he hike due west?

A. 18 miles

B. 24 miles

C. 32 miles

D. 44 miles

4. The high school band director builds a platform so that he can see the formations the marching band creates. How long is the longest support beam? Round your answer to the nearest foot.

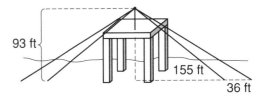

A. 124 ft

B. 142 feet

C. 160 feet

D. 185 feet

MN Test Prep Grade 11

5. The bottom of a 45-foot ladder is placed against a building so the top of the ladder reaches the top of a 30-foot high window. How far from the base of the building is the bottom of the ladder? Round your answer to the nearest tenth.

   A. 5.6 ft

   B. 33.5 ft

   C. 35.3 ft

   D. 212.5 ft

6. Sheila and Janet are decorating a 10-ft by 14-ft room with streamers for a birthday party. If they want to connect the corners of the room diagonally, what is the smallest length of streamers that Sheila and Janet need? Round your answer to the nearest foot.

   A. 10 ft   **C.** 17 ft

   B. 12 ft   **D.** 96 ft

7. The length of a rectangle is 13 more than the width. If the length of the diagonal is 65 units, what is the area of the rectangle?

   A. 39 square units

   B. 52 square units

   C. 1521 square units

   D. 2028 square units

8. The length of the diagonal of one of the bases of a cube is $15\sqrt{2}$ inches. What is the surface area of the cube?

   A. 30 in^3

   B. 180 in^3

   C. 225 in^3

   D. 1350 in^3

Gridded Response: Fill in the grid with your answer to each question.

9. The members of the color guard sew their own flags. They create a flag in the shape of a right triangle with a hypotenuse of length $15\sqrt{2}$ m. The area of the flag uses 4 m^2 of material. What is the length of the shortest leg of the flag? Round your answer to the nearest hundredth of a meter.

Extended Response: Show your work for each question.

10. Solve the following problems.

    A. Two different triangles are shown below. What is the length of $\overline{XY}$? Write your answer in simplest radical form and as a rational number rounded to the nearest tenth of a foot.

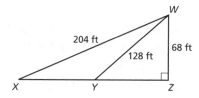

    B. A right triangle has one leg that is half as long as the other. The area of the triangle is 36 square units. What is the length of each leg and the hypotenuse of the triangle? Round the answer to the nearest hundredth.

SPATIAL SENSE, GEOMETRY, AND MEASUREMENT

Right Triangle Trigonometry

> B3 Know and use properties of two- and three-dimensional figures to solve real-world and mathematical problems such as: finding area, perimeter, volume, and surface area; applying direct or indirect methods of measurement; the Pythagorean theorem and its converse; and properties of 45°-45°-90° and 30°-60°-90° triangles.

Select the best answer for each question.

1. Wendell is building a wheelchair ramp for the front steps at his grandparents' home. The angle of elevation needs to be 7°. The height of the stairs is 3.5 feet. How long is the ramp?

   A. 3.5 feet

   B. 5.3 feet

   C. 18.4 feet

   D. 28.7 feet

2. A baseball diamond is a square as shown in the picture. What is the distance from first base, labeled as 1, to third base, labeled as 3?

   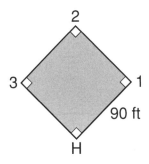

   A. 45 feet

   B. 90 feet

   C. $90\sqrt{2}$ feet

   D. $100\sqrt{2}$ feet

3. A regular pentagon has sides 30 cm long. A circle is inscribed. Which equation can be used to solve for the radius, *r*, of the circle?

   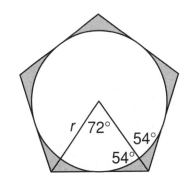

   A. $\dfrac{r}{\sin 54°} = \dfrac{15}{\sin 45°}$

   B. $\dfrac{r}{\sin 54°} = \dfrac{30}{\sin 45°}$

   C. $\dfrac{r}{\sin 54°} = \dfrac{30}{\sin 72°}$

   D. $\dfrac{r}{\sin 72°} = \dfrac{30}{\sin 54°}$

4. Which expression can be used to determine the measure of *a*?

   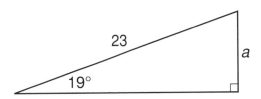

   A. $23\cos 19°$

   B. $19\cos 23°$

   C. $23\sin 19°$

   D. $19\sin 19°$

MN Test Prep Grade 11

5. What is the length of the ladder?

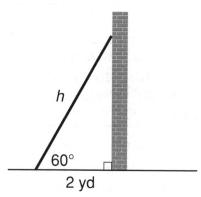

2 yd

A. 0.25

B. 0.50

C. $\sqrt{3}$

D. 4

6. The length of a rectangle is double its width. Which ratio would you use to find the angle formed by the diagonal and the length of the rectangle?

A. $\sin \theta = \dfrac{1}{2}$

B. $\cos \theta = \dfrac{1}{2}$

C. $\tan \theta = \dfrac{1}{2}$

D. $\tan \theta = 2$

Gridded Response: Fill in the grid with your answer to each question.

7. A lighthouse is 65 feet above sea level. From the top of the lighthouse, Angelo spots his kayak on the ground. The angle of depression to the kayak is 14°. What is the distance in feet that Angelo must travel from the base of the lighthouse to the kayak in order to retrieve the kayak?

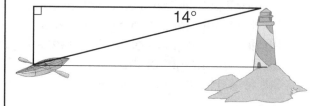

Extended Response: Show your work for each question.

8. An airplane with a ground speed of 280 miles per hour is trying to fly due North. The pilot notices the plane's northern velocity is only 240 miles per hour. By how many degrees is the plane being blown off course? Round your answer to the nearest degree.

9. The equation $(\sin A)^2 + (\cos A)^2 = 1$ is known as a Pythagorean Identity, and is true for all values of A.

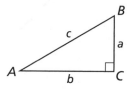

A. Write $\sin A$ and $\cos A$ in terms of a, b, and c.

B. Use your results from part a to prove the identity
$$(\sin A)^2 + (\cos A)^2 = 1$$

MN Test Prep Grade 11

SPATIAL SENSE, GEOMETRY, AND MEASUREMENT

Measure Using Tools

B7,B8 Perform basic constructions with a straightedge and compass.
Draw accurate representations of planar figures using a variety of tools.

Select the best answer for each question.

1. Which is the most precise measurement?

   A. 3 yards   C. 16 miles

   B. 725 feet   D. 4 inches

2. Which measurement is the least precise?

   A. 62 kilometers

   B. 5 meters

   C. 23 centimeters

   D. 2 millimeters

3. Which is the most precise measurement for the weight of a bag of oranges?

   A. 10 pounds

   B. $11\frac{1}{2}$ pounds

   C. $11\frac{3}{4}$ pounds

   D. 12 pounds

4. Which is the most precise measurement for the capacity of a milk container?

   A. 1.89 liters

   B. 1.9 liters

   C. 2 liters

   D. 1,955 milliliters

5. The table shows the heights of four mountains in Alaska. Which heights have four significant digits?

Mountain	Height (in feet)
Blackburn	16,390
Foraker	17,400
Hunter	14,573
McKinley	20,320

   A. Blackburn and Foraker

   B. Blackburn and McKinley

   C. Foraker and Hunter

   D. Hunter and McKinley

6. A hummingbird egg is 0.013 meters long. How many significant digits are in this measurement?

   A. 2   C. 4

   B. 3   D. 13

7. Nick stated that he weighs 75 kilograms. What is the range of his possible weight?

   A. 70 kilograms to 80 kilograms

   B. 74.1 kilograms to 75.9 kilograms

   C. 74.5 kilograms to 75.5 kilograms

   D. 74.9 kilograms to 75.1 kilograms

8. These four weights were all used to describe an elephant. Which weight has 3 significant digits?

A. 12,000 pounds   C. 12,395 pounds

B. 12,390 pounds   D. 12,400 pounds

9. Which shows the perimeter of this rectangle with the correct number of significant digits?

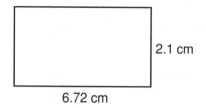

2.1 cm

6.72 cm

A. 17.6 centimeters

B. 17.64 centimeters

C. 17.7 centimeters

D. 18 centimeters

10. In one park there are markers at the end of each 0.25-mile section of a hiking trail. There are 14 markers in all. Using the correct number of significant digits, what is the length of the trail?

A. 3.5 miles   C. 4 miles

B. 3.50 miles   D. 4.0 miles

11. A car travels 314.8 miles on 12.8 gallons of gas. Using the correct number of significant digits, what is the car's fuel efficiency in miles per gallon?

A. 24.5 miles per gallon

B. 24.59 miles per gallon

C. 24.59375 miles per gallon

D. 24.6 miles per gallon

12. The formula for converting Fahrenheit to Celsius temperatures is $C = \frac{5}{9}(F - 32)$. Using the correct number of significant digits, what is 72°F in degrees Celsius?

A. 20°C   C. 22.2°C

B. 22°C   D. 22.222…°C

Gridded Response: Fill in the grid with your answer to each question.

13. What is the length of the drawing of a fly, rounded to the nearest centimeter? 1 inch = 2.5 centimeter.

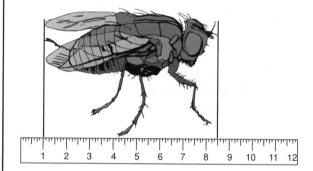

Extended Response: Show your work for each question.

14. When measuring the length of a foot, what units would be more precise, mm or m ? Explain.

Name_____ Date _____ Class_____

SPATIAL SENSE, GEOMETRY, AND MEASUREMENT

Coordinate Geometry

B5, B1 Use coordinate geometry to represent and examine geometric concepts such as the distance between two points, the midpoint of a line segment, the slope of a line, and the slopes of parallel and perpendicular lines. Know and use theorems about triangles and parallel lines in elementary geometry to justify facts about various geometrical figures and solve real-world and mathematical problems. These theorems include criteria for two triangles to be congruent or similar and facts about parallel lines cut by a transversal.

Select the best answer for each question.

Use the graph to answer questions 1 and 2.

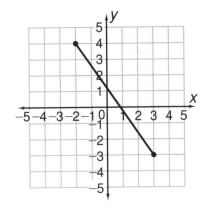

1. What is one quarter of the length of the segment shown in the graph?

   A. $\dfrac{\sqrt{2}}{4}$

   B. $\dfrac{7\sqrt{2}}{4}$

   C. $\dfrac{\sqrt{74}}{4}$

   D. $\dfrac{\sqrt{87}}{4}$

2. Find the coordinates of the midpoint of the line segment shown in the graph.

   A. (0, 0)

   B. (0.5, 0.5)

   C. (0.5, 1)

   D. (1, 0)

Use the map to answer questions 3–5.

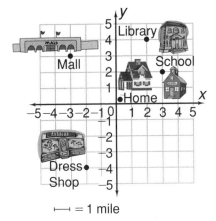

⊢——⊣ = 1 mile

3. Jeni drives straight from school to the dress shop. How far does she travel? Round your answer to the nearest tenth.

   A. 5.6 miles

   B. 6.9 miles

   C. 7.8 miles

   D. 8.7 miles

MN Test Prep Grade 11

4. One Saturday, Jeni drives straight from home to the library to study. After studying, she then drives straight to the mall. After shopping at the mall, she drives home. How many miles did Jeni drive? Round your answer to the nearest tenth.

   A. 4.5 miles

   B. 9.6 miles

   C. 11.8 miles

   D. 13.8 miles

5. The gas station lies exactly in the middle of the straight line that connects the school and the dress shop. What are the coordinates of the gas station?

   A. (0, 1)

   B. (0, −1)

   C. (0.5, −1)

   D. (1, 2)

6. The distance between point (1, 5) and point (4, c) is 5. Find c.

   A. 1 or 9

   B. −2 or 9

   C. 1 or −9

   D. −1 or 9

7. The midpoint between point A and the point (−2, −7) is (20, 15). What are the coordinates of point A?

   A. (3, 30)

   B. (23, −2)

   C. (38, 23)

   D. (42, 37)

Gridded Response: Fill in the grid with your answer to each question.

8. What is the negative of the slope of the line shown in the graph?

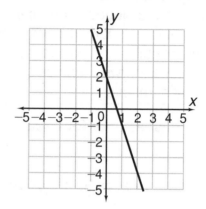

Extended Response: Show your work for each question.

9. B is the midpoint of segment AC. If $B = \left(\dfrac{1}{6}, \dfrac{1}{3}\right)$ and $A = \left(\dfrac{5}{6}, \dfrac{1}{3}\right)$, what is the absolute value of the x-coordinate of point C?

MN Test Prep Grade 11

SPATIAL SENSE, GEOMETRY, AND MEASUREMENT

Mathematical Reasoning and Proof

> B3 Know and use properties of two- and three-dimensional figures to solve real-world and mathematical problems such as: finding area, perimeter, volume, and surface area; applying direct or indirect methods of measurement; the Pythagorean theorem and its converse; and properties of 45°-45°-90° and 30°-60°-90° triangles

Select the best answer for each question.

1. For which statement is the diagram a counterexample?

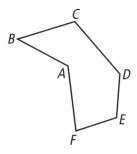

   A. Every hexagon has 6 sides.
   B. The sum of the interior angles in a hexagon is 720°.
   C. An irregular hexagon has at least one side that is not congruent to the other sides.
   D. A polygon cannot contain a reflex angle.

2. Which statement is the best example of inductive reasoning?

   A. All of the dogs that came to the veterinary clinic today had fleas, so all dogs must have fleas.
   B. When I added 10,000 pairs of even numbers, the sum was even each time. The sum of any pair of even numbers is even.
   C. It is rainy today, so I think it will rain next week.
   D. All dogs have four legs. My pet has four legs so he must be a dog.

3. Which statement is the best example of deductive reasoning?

   A. On a bookcase, there are 16 books on the top shelf and 8 books on the bottom shelf. Since, there are no other books on the bookcase, there are 24 books in the bookcase.
   B. Alexander enjoys reading. One day he will be an author.
   C. All birds have wings. A blue jay has wings, so it must be a bird.
   D. The southern states are popular travel destinations.

MN Test Prep Grade 11

4. Which statement is a counterexample for the following conjecture? Each interior angle in a quadrilateral is 90°.

A. A square has 4 interior angles, each of which measures 90°.

B. Bob drew a parallelogram with interior angles that measure 100°, 80°, 100°, and 80°.

C. A rectangle has four 90° angles.

D. Rectangles and squares are parallelograms.

5. For which statement would you use deductive reasoning?

A. The sum of the exterior angles of a polygon is 360°.

B. Positive numbers are used more frequently than negative numbers.

C. It has rained every April in the last 5 years so it will rain next April too.

D. A triangle can have many different shapes.

6. Which is the best argument for the claim, "I will pass my next math test"?

A. Jen says, "I have done well on the last five math tests."

B. Mary says, "I like math."

C. Heath says, "When I did the review questions, I got most of the answers correct."

D. Jorge says, "My parents think I will do well in math this year."

7. Which word or phrase best describes the following statement?

Kate sleeps 8 h every night. She rides the bus 1.6 h each way to work every day for five days. So, Kate spends the equivalent of one awake day riding the bus each week.

A. Conjecture

B. Inductive reasoning

C. Deductive reasoning

D. Counterexample

Gridded Response: Fill in the grid with your answer to each question.

8. The total surface area of a closed box is 322 square feet. The box is 8 feet high and has a square base and lid. What is the length in feet of the side of the base?

Extended Response: Show your work for each question.

9. Lauren, Megan, Avery, Marie, and Elizabeth are friends. Use the clues to arrange the girls in order from oldest to youngest.

I   Lauren is younger than Marie.

II At least three girls are older than Avery.

III Avery is not the youngest.

IV Megan is older than Marie and younger than Elizabeth.

SPATIAL SENSE, GEOMETRY, AND MEASUREMENT

Polygons

> B3 Know and use properties of two- and three-dimensional figures to solve real-world and mathematical problems such as: finding area, perimeter, volume, and surface area; applying direct or indirect methods of measurement; the Pythagorean theorem and its converse; and properties of 45°-45°-90° and 30°-60°-90° triangles

Select the best answer for each question.

1. Three of the interior angles of a quadrilateral measure 104.9°, 74.2°, and 55.6°. What is the measure of the fourth interior angle?

   A. 123.5°

   B. 132.5°

   C. 125.3°

   D. 153.2°

2. What is the measure of an interior angle in a regular dodecagon?

   A. 150°

   B. 165°

   C. 135°

   D. 112.5°

3. The sum of the interior angle measures of a polygon is 3600°. How many sides does the polygon have?

   A. 21

   B. 22

   C. 23

   D. 24

4. The measures of two interior angles in a scalene triangle are 34.5° and 70.2°. Find the measures of the exterior angles for this triangle.

   A. 104.6°, 109.8°, 144.5°

   B. 104.7°, 109.8°, 145.5°

   C. 104.7°, 109.9°, 145.5°

   D. 105°, 110°, 146°

5. Find the sum of the interior angle measures of this polygon.

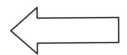

   A. 360°

   B. 540°

   C. 720°

   D. 900°

6. Which phrase BEST describes this figure?

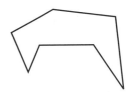

   A. concave heptagon

   B. regular heptagon

   C. convex nonagon

   D. regular nonagon

MN Test Prep Grade 11

7. The measures of the exterior angles at four vertices of a pentagon are 43.7°, 122.2°, 35.1° and 88.9°. Find the measure of the exterior angle at the fifth vertex.

    A. 67.4°

    B. 69.9°

    C. 325.8°

    D. 70.1°

8. A polygon has 14 sides. What is the sum of the interior angles?

    A. 2160°

    B. 2340°

    C. 2520°

    D. 2700°

9. Find z.

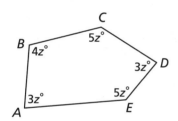

    A. 15

    B. 27

    C. 35

    D. 42

Gridded Response: Fill in the grid with your answer to each question.

10. A regular polygon has 114 sides. Find the measure of each interior angle. Round to the nearest degree.

Extended Response: Show your work for each question.

11. Show that *EFGH* is a parallelogram given $s = 5$ and $t = 6$.

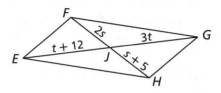

12. Two exterior angles of a parallelogram measure 2.9° and 177.1°. What are the measures of the interior angles of the parallelogram?

13. A regular polygon has 114 sides. Find the measure of each interior angle.

14. A polygon has six sides, each 24 cm long. Four interior angles measure 60° and two interior angles measure 240°. Classify this polygon according to its sides and angles.

MN Test Prep Grade 11

Name_____ Date _____ Class_____

SPATIAL SENSE, GEOMETRY, AND MEASUREMENT

Transformations

B6 Use numeric, graphic, and symbolic representations of transformations such as reflections, translations, and change of scale in one, two, and three dimensions to solve real-world and mathematical problems.

Select the best answer for each question.

1. Which type of transformation is shown below?

   A. translation

   B. rotation

   C. reflection

   D. glide reflection

2. What are the coordinates of point A when $\triangle ABC$ is dilated by a scale factor of 0.5?

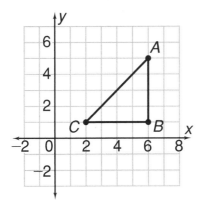

   A. (6, 5)

   B. (3, 2.5)

   C. (3, 0.5)

   D. (1, 0.5)

3. The figure is symmetric. The line of symmetry is shown as a dotted line. Find the coordinates of point A.

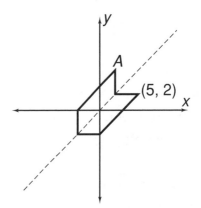

   A. (−5, −2)

   B. (2, 5)

   C. (−2, −5)

   D. (2, −5)

MN Test Prep Grade 11

Name_____ Date _____ Class_____

4. What is the degree of rotation about the origin from figure *A* to figure *B*?

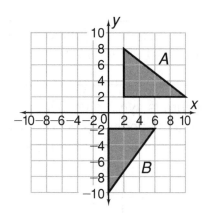

   A. 45° counter clockwise

   B. 90° counter clockwise

   C. 180° counter clockwise

   D. 270° counter clockwise

5. Which transformation changes the size of a figure?

   A. dilation

   B. rotation

   C. reflection

   D. glide reflection

6. How many lines of symmetry does a regular pentagon have?

   A. 1

   B. 2

   C. 3

   D. 5

Gridded Response: Fill in the grid with your answer to each question.

7. Triangle *XYZ* has vertices $X(-5, -9)$, $Y(-4, -5)$, and $Z(-7, -8)$.

   A. What is the *x*-coordinate of point *X* after it is reflected across the *y*-axis?

   B. What is the absolute value of the *y*-coordinate of point *Z* after a 270° rotation about the origin?

Extended Response: Show your work for each question.

8. Complete the figure so that it is symmetric.

MN Test Prep Grade 11

Name_____ Date_____ Class_____

SAMPLE TEST A

Select the best answer for each question.

1. If C is a 5×6 matrix and D is a 6×3 matrix, what are the dimensions of DC?

  A. not defined

  B. 5×6

  C. 6×6

  D. 5×3

2. What is the vertical shift factor in the equation $f(x) = a2^{bx - c} + d$?

  A. a

  B. b

  C. c

  D. d

3. Find the y-intercept of the line that passes through the point $(-2, 0)$ and is perpendicular to the line shown in the graph.

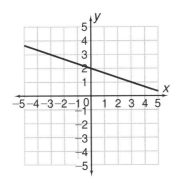

  A. $(0, 6)$

  B. $(0, -2)$

  C. $(0, 2)$

  D. $(0, 4)$

4. Which bar graph correctly represents the data in the table?

Fruit	Day 1	Day 2
Bananas	16	22
Kiwi	8	6
Mango	24	18
Oranges	40	50
Apples	52	50

A.

Fruit Sold

B.

Fruit Sold

C.

Fruit Sold

D.

Fruit Sold

5. Which of the following is a factor of $3x^2 + 23x + 14$?

  A. $(x + 8)$

  B. $(x + 9)$

  C. $(3x + 1)$

  D. $(3x + 2)$

Sample Test A Grade 11

6. What is the slope of the line that passes through the points (2, 4) and (1, 2)?

A. -2

B. $-\dfrac{1}{2}$

C. $\dfrac{1}{2}$

D. 2

7. Suppose point Q is translated to the right 2 units and down 5 units. What rule describes the translation?

A. $(x, y) \rightarrow (x + 2, y - 5)$

B. $(x, y) \rightarrow (x - 2, y + 5)$

C. $(x, y) \rightarrow (x + 5, y - 2)$

D. $(x, y) \rightarrow (x - 2, y - 5)$

8. The volume formula for a sphere is given below, where r is the radius. What is the volume of a sphere when it has a diameter of 10 m? Round the answer to the tenth place.

$$V = \frac{4}{3}\pi r^3$$

A. 388.8

B. 523.6

C. 646.0

D. 4188.8

9. Craig earns $200 per week plus 8% commission on sales. Joan earns $150 per week plus 12% commission on sales. Last week, both had sales of $1500. Who earned more money?

A. Craig earned more than Joan

B. Joan earned more than Craig

C. Both earned the same amount

D. Cannot be determined

10. A radio station surveyed its listeners to determine the ages of its listeners. The results are shown below in the stem-and-leaf plot.

Stem	Leaf (Key: 3|2 = 32)
0	8 8 9
1	0 1 3 4 4 6 6 8 8 9
2	0 0 0 4 8 9
3	2 3 4 5 6 6 8 9 9
4	4 5
5	2 7 9
6	1 2 8

What is the mean age of the listeners of the radio station rounded to the nearest whole number?

A. 18   C 25

B. 20   D. 30

11. A rectangle has an area of 253 square yards. The length is 12 yards longer than the width. What is the width?

A. 8 yards   C. 17 yards

B. 11 yards   D. 20 yards

12. Let $f(x) = 5(x - 2)^2 + 3$. If you wanted to shift the graph of the function up, what would you do?

A. Change 5 to 3

B. Change 3 to 5

C. Change 5 to 6

D. Change 2 to 6

Sample Test A Grade 11

13. Which figure can be made from this net?

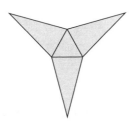

- **A.** cone
- **B.** triangular prism
- **C.** triangular pyramid
- **D.** cylinder

14. If the equation $HP = -6x^2 + 48x$ is the approximation of the horsepower developed by an engine operating at x thousand revolutions per minute (RPM),at what RPM is maximum horsepower reached?

- **A.** 6
- **B.** 3
- **C.** 4
- **D.** 24

15. Which method describes a stratified random sample?

- **A.** Henry asks his neighbors who they will vote for in the next election.
- **B.** Henry phones every 100th person in the phone book and asks who they will vote for in the next election.
- **C.** Henry randomly samples 1000 males and 1000 females and asks who they will vote for in the next election.
- **D.** Both B and C are examples of stratified random samples.

16. Name the model that the graph of $y = a^x + b$ represents.

- **A.** Quadratic
- **B.** Exponential Growth
- **C.** Exponential Decay
- **D.** Linear

17. Which word or phrase best describes the following statement?

Sean stated that the interior angles in a hexagon are always obtuse. I drew a hexagon with 5 interior angles that measured 130° and one interior angle that measured 70°, so Sean's statement is false.

- **A.** Conjecture
- **B.** Inductive reasoning
- **C.** Deductive reasoning
- **D.** Counterexample

18. What is the equation of the function that matches the table?

x	−3	0	3	6
y	2	4	6	8

- **A.** $y = -\dfrac{2}{3}x$
- **C.** $y = \dfrac{1}{3}x + 3$
- **B.** $y = 2x + 4$
- **D.** $y = \dfrac{2}{3}x + 4$

19. What is NOT true for two lines that are parallel to each other, but NOT on top of each other?

- **A.** They do not intersect each other.
- **B.** The system will have no solution.
- **C.** If you extend the lines you will see the intersection.
- **D.** All of the above are true.

Sample Test A Grade 11

20. What is the volume of a cone with a height of 14 cm and a base diameter of 18 cm?

A. 874.3 cm^3 **C.** 1187.5 cm^3

B. 1029 cm^3 **D.** 1651.5 cm^3

21. There are 12 blocks in a bag. There are 4 red blocks, 4 green blocks, and 4 blue blocks. You pick out three blocks. Each time a block is picked, it is NOT replaced back into the bag. What is the probability of choosing 3 green blocks?

A. $\dfrac{1}{9}$ **C.** $\dfrac{1}{55}$

B. $\dfrac{1}{36}$ **D.** $\dfrac{1}{81}$

22. Solve the equation:

$$|5x - 10| + 5 = 15$$

A. 0, 4   **C.** 0

B. 1, 5   **D.** no solution

23. Members of the Ram's Booster Club are designing a calendar of the school year to sell as a fund raiser. They begin by making a roster of the possible number of days in a month. Which shows the roster?

A. {30, 31}

B. {x| 28 < x ≤ 31}

C. {28, 29, 30, 31}

D. {x| x ≥ 28 and x ∈ N}

24. One of the interior angles of a parallelogram measures 82°. What is the measure of the opposite angle?

A. 8°   **C.** 82°

B. 98°   **D.** 180°

25. Evaluate $10^4 \times 10^{-3} \div 10^2$.

A. 10^{-9}

B. 10^{-1}

C. 10^1

D. 10^9

26. An ad for interlocking foam squares is shown below. A teacher has 2 packages of red, 6 packages of blue, and half a package of yellow squares. He wants to build a rectangle so that each row is the same color. What can be the maximum number of squares per row?

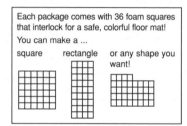

Each package comes with 36 foam squares that interlock for a safe, colorful floor mat! You can make a ...
square   rectangle   or any shape you want!

A. 2

B. 6

C. 18

D. 36

27. Which of the following would you expect to have a positive correlation?

A. The height of a person versus their number of toes on their feet

B. Years of education versus salary earned

C. Age of a car versus the value of the car

D. Color of hair versus grade in math

Sample Test A Grade 11

28. $\triangle ABC \cong \triangle DEF$. $AB = 2x - 10$ and $DE = x + 20$. Find x.

    A. 10   **C.** 30

    B. 20   **D.** 40

29. Terry's TVs calculates their profit using the equation $p = 0.4\sqrt{c} - 125$ where p is the profit, and c is the wholesale cost. If they make a profit of $375 on one TV, what is the wholesale cost of the TV sold?

    A. $1,250

    B. $1,512,550

    C. $1,562,500

    D. $1,937,250

30. What is the common difference for the given arithmetic sequence?

$$23, 19, 15, 11, 7, \ldots$$

    A. Subtract 3.

    B. Divide by 2.

    C. Divide by 5.

    D. Subtract 4.

31. Given $y = a^3 + 2b + cd$, what is the value of y when $a = 1$, $b = 2$, $c = 3$ and $d = 4$?

    A. 9

    B. 17

    C. 34

    D. 68

32. Two angles are supplementary. The measure of one angle is 6 more than triple the other angle. What are the angles?

    A. 43.5° and 46.5°

    B. 43.5° and 136.5°

    C. 58° and 122°

    D. 58° and 32°

33. A new school was asked to determine its mascot. The school had 5 choices: grizzly bear, bull dog, bald eagle, wildcat, or panther. The students were polled by the school newspaper as to which mascot they would vote for. The table shows the results of the poll.

Mascot	Number of Votes
Grizzly Bear	68
Bull Dog	12
Bald Eagle	24
Wildcat	44
Panther	52

What is the probability that a student will vote for the mascot to be a wildcat?

    A. $\dfrac{3}{50}$

    B. $\dfrac{11}{50}$

    C. $\dfrac{13}{50}$

    D. $\dfrac{17}{50}$

Sample Test A Grade 11

34. Which part in the quadratic equation is the discriminant?

    A. $-b$

    B. $b^2 - 4ac$

    C. $2a$

    D. $\sqrt{b^2 - 4ac}$

35. The two equal sides of an isosceles triangle are 25 inches. The angle between the two equal sides is 40°. Find the length of the third side, to the nearest inch.

    A. 17.1

    B. 23.2

    C. 31

    D. 46.5

36. Which of the following lines is the steepest with the listed points on each line?

    A. Line 1: (2, 3), (3, 7)

    B. Line 2: (3, 8) (4, 6)

    C. Line 3: (−1, 2) (7, 19)

    D. Line 4: (4, 6) (5, 0)

37. The bending of a beam varies directly as the mass of the load it supports. Suppose that a beam is bent 18 mm by a mass of 90 kg. How much will the beam bend when it supports a mass of 205 kg?

    A. 17 mm

    B. 23 mm

    C. 41 mm

    D. 102 mm

38. In the United States, about 229,000,000 people speak English. In Canada, about 18,000,000 people speak English. What is the total number of English speaking people in the United States and Canada?

    A. 2.11×10^8

    B. 2.11×10^9

    C. 2.47×10^8

    D. 2.47×10^9

39. The dollar amount of the total purchases from a corner kiosk over a 3-month period is shown below for 21 randomly selected individuals.

$10	$18	$10	$22	$14	$41	$31
$43	$8	$6	$27	$18	$27	$32
$5	$53	$30	$25	$30	$22	$42

What is the interquartile range?

    A. 15

    B. 19.5

    C. 21

    D. 25

Sample Test A Grade 11

40. Which of the following best describes this statement, "The opposite angles of a trapezoid are supplementary"?

   A. Sometimes

   B. Always

   C. Never

   D. Not enough information to answer

41. Given that $f(x) = 6x - 21$ and $g(x) = x^3 - 7x$, determine $(g \circ f)(3)$.

   A. -15 **C.** 6

   B. -6 **D.** 15

42. The members of the color guard sew their own flags. They create a flag in the shape of a right triangle with a hypotenuse of length $5\sqrt{2}$ m. The area of the flag uses 4 m² of material. What is the length of the shortest leg of the flag?

   A. 1 m

   B. 2 m

   C. 4 m

   D. 6 m

43. Which of the following expressions is NOT equivalent to the other three?

   A. $\dfrac{4x^2}{x^2 - 3x} \cdot \dfrac{2x - 6}{8y^2}$

   B. $\dfrac{6xy^2}{x^2} \div \dfrac{3y^4}{2x^2}$

   C. $\dfrac{10x^4y}{5xy^2} \div 2x^2y$

   D. $\dfrac{4x}{xy^2 + 2y^2} \cdot \dfrac{x^2 - 4}{4x - 8}$

44. What is the difference, to the nearest degree Fahrenheit, between the annual mean coastal water temperature of St. Petersburg and the annual mean coastal water temperature of Newport?

	Jan	Feb	Mar	Apr	May	Jun
St.Petersberg	62°	64°	68°	74°	80°	84°
Newport	37°	36°	37°	46°	55°	62°

	Jul	Aug	Sep	Oct	Nov	Dec
St.Petersberg	86°	86°	84°	78°	70°	64°
Newport	68°	70°	67°	60°	52°	44°

   A. 17

   B. 22

   C. 24

   D. 30

45. Determine whether the point $(3, -8)$ is located on the graph $y = x^2 - 5x + 14$.

   A. Yes, the point is on the graph.

   B. The point is not on the graph.

   C. There is not enough information.

   D. The graph passes through the point more than once.

46. The equal interior angle measures in an isosceles triangle are double the non-equal angle measure. What are the measures of the angles?

   A. 36°, 72°, 72°

   B. 45°, 90°, 90°

   C. 72°, 36°, 36°

   D. 90°, 45°, 45°

Sample Test A Grade 11

47. If $f(x) = x^4 + 3x^2 + 2$, what would be the best way to describe $3f(x)$, in relation to $f(x)$.

- **A.** A vertical reflection
- **B.** A horizontal reflection
- **C.** A horizontal stretch
- **D.** A vertical stretch

48. Which account earns the most simple interest after 1 year? Assume that interest is paid annually.

- **A.** $4000 at 10.2% per year
- **B.** $5000 at 8% per year
- **C.** $8000 at 4.6% per year
- **D.** $10,000 at 4% per year

49. Which questions are biased?

- **I** What is your favorite type of food?
- **II** What is your favorite type of food: pizza, hamburgers, fried chicken, or other?

- **A.** I is biased
- **B.** II is biased
- **C.** I and II are biased
- **D.** None of the above are biased

50. Cara's family rented a car for their 3-day vacation to the Grand Canyon. They paid $29.00 per day and $0.12 for each mile driven. Which expression represents Cara's family's cost to rent the car for 3 days and drive 318 miles?

- **A.** 3[9 + 0.12(318)]
- **B.** 29 + 0.12(318)
- **C.** 29 + 3 + 0.12 + 318
- **D.** 29(3) + 0.12(318)

51. Which of these functions is linear?

- **A.** $y = \cos x$
- **B.** $y - 3x = 4x + 15 + 13y$
- **C.** $y = 3x^2 - 1$
- **D.** $y^2 = 2x + 4$

52. Suppose the side length of a square is doubled. By what factor is its area increased?

- **A.** $\dfrac{1}{2}$
- **B.** $\dfrac{\sqrt{2}}{2}$
- **C.** 2
- **D.** 4

53. Which absolute value equation has the solution shown here?

- **A.** $|x - 3| > 5$
- **B.** $|x - 3| < 5$
- **C.** $|x - 3| = 5$
- **D** $|x - 3| \le 5$

54. What is the approximate area of this triangle?

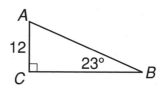

- **A.** 72 square units
- **B.** 123 square units
- **C.** 170 square units
- **D.** 186 square units

Sample Test A Grade 11

55. Which statement is true?

   A. The closer together the points on a scatter plot are, the more reliable the predictions.

   B. The closer together the points on a scatter plot are, the stronger the correlation.

   C. The closer together the points on a scatter plot are, the higher the correlation coefficient.

   D All of the above are true.

56. In parallelogram $ABCD$, side $\overline{AB}$ is parallel to side $\overline{CD}$. The measure of $\angle ABC = 76°$. What is the measure of $\angle BCD$?

   A. 76°

   B. 14°

   C. 104°

   D. 180°

57. Each square represents 0.02 probability. The squares with A represent the probability that event A occurs. The Z represents the probability that event Z occurs. The area where the two letters overlap represents the probability that both events occur. What is the probability that event A occurs?

A	A	A	A	A
	A	A	A	Z
	Z	Z	Z	Z
A	A	A	Z	Z
A	Z	Z	Z	A
AZ	AZ	A	AZ	A
AZ	AZ	AZ	Z	Z
A	A	Z	Z	AZ
AZ		A	Z	AZ
A	Z	AZ	A	AZ

   A. 0.17

   B. 0.35

   C. 0.5

   D. 0.62

58. A 4-month-old baby weighs 18.4 pounds. What does the baby weigh in grams? 1 pound = 0.45 kilogram.

   A. 8181 grams

   B. 8280 grams

   C. 40,889 grams

   D. 4089 grams

Sample Test A Grade 11

59. What is the *y*-intercept for
$7x^2 = y + 7$?

A. 7

B. 12

C. 2

D. −7

60. How many diagonals does a pentagon have?

A. 5

B. 6

C. 7

D. 8

61. How many perfect squares lie between 2 and 33?

A. 0   **C.** 4

B. 3   **D.** 5

62. Which of the following polynomials is an upward opening parabola?

A. $y = \left(x^2\right)^2$

B. $y = (x + 2)(x + 3)(x + 4)$

C. $y = -x^2 + 5x - 9$

D. $y = -x^4 + 1000$

63. What is the slope of the line passing through the points whose coordinates are listed in the table?

x	−2	−1	0	1	2
y	5	2	−1	−4	−7

A. −3

B. 0

C. $\dfrac{1}{3}$

D. undefined

64. The points (1, 2) and (7, 2) form the shorter leg of a right triangle. The area of the triangle is 24 square units. One endpoint of the longer leg of the right triangle is (7, 2). Which is one possibility for the other endpoint of the longer leg?

A. (−7, −10)

B. (0, −2)

C. (7, −6)

D. (8, −2)

65. What is the *x*-intercept for
$7x^2 = y + 7$?

A. −1

B. 1

C. 2

D. Both A and B are correct

66. Find the first quartile of the data below.

2, 4, 5, 7, 9, 11, 17, 22, 37, 57, 69

A. 5

B. 11

C. 18

D. 24

67. Which of the following is the best estimate for π?

A. 3.14

B. 3.1415

C. 3.1425

D. 3.145

68. Can a quadratic function have degree three?

    A. Yes

    B. No

    C. Sometimes

    D. It cannot be determined.

69. Manuel drinks 362 milliliters of organic orange juice every day. About how many fluid ounces does he drink in seven days? 28.4 milliliters = 1 fluid ounce.

    A. 14.5 fluid ounces

    B. 43.25 fluid ounces

    C. 54.125 fluid ounces

    D. 89.23 fluid ounces

70. The following equation is an example of which property?

$$4.7(5.1x - 9.2y) = 4.7(5.1x) - 4.7(9.2y)$$

    A. Associative Property

    B. Distributive Property

    C. Commutative Property

    D. Identity Property

71. Which of the number sentences below is false?

    A. $-3.43 > -3.41$

    B. $-\dfrac{3}{4} > -\sqrt{2}$

    C. $-\sqrt{16} > -\sqrt{25}$

    D. $-\pi < -\sqrt{\dfrac{25}{16}}$

72. Rebecca has to simplify the following expression on a test.

$$\frac{22 + 6^3 - 5 \cdot 3 - 4^2 + 12}{3}$$

What is her second step?

    A. Compute $22 + 216$

    B. Compute 4^2

    C. Add 12

    D. Compute $216 - 11$

73. In one row of Jayne's garden, she plants five tomato seeds. She then continues the row with five watermelon seeds. How long must the row be to plant these 10 seeds? Hint: The plants need adequate spacing at the beginning and end of a row.

Type of Seed	Spacing Needed between Seeds
Tomato	30 inches
Broccoli	24 inches
Onion	3 inches
Cauliflower	$1\frac{1}{4}$ feet
Watermelon	6 feet

    A. 51 ft

    B. 180 ft

    C. 42 ft 6 in.

    D. 32 ft 9 in.

Sample Test A Grade 11

74. Triangle *XYZ* has vertices *X*(−5, −9), *Y*(−4, −5), and *Z*(−7, −8). What is the *y*-coordinate of point *Y* after it is reflected across the *x*-axis?

A. −2

B. 3

C. 2

D. 5

75. Which ordered pair represents the solution to the following linear system?

$y = 3x - 7$
$y = -x + 5$

A. $(3, 2)$

B. $(-3, -2)$

C. $(2, 3)$

D. $(2, -3)$

76. A rubber ball has a diameter of 6 inches. If a basketball has a diameter three times as large, determine the volume of the basketball. (Use $\pi = 3.14$, round to the nearest hundredth if necessary.)

A. 890.32 in^3

B. 2289.06 in^3

C. 1156.46 in^3

D. 3052.08 in^3

77. What is 24% of 321?

A. 37.67

B. 77.04

C. 122.04

D. 215.76

78. What is the missing value for the table to have an inverse relationship?

x	3	5	8
y	7	?	1.2

A. 20

B. 18

C. 5

D. 15

79. What is the value of the expression $\dfrac{6x^3 y}{5y^{-4}}$ when *x* is −2 and *y* is 3?

A. $\dfrac{15}{32}$

B. $\dfrac{211}{32}$

C. −3375

D. −2332.8

80. A semi-cylindrical tunnel 30 m diameter and 1200 m long is drilled through a mountain to route trains. 423,900 cubic meters of rock and dirt were drilled from the tunnel. A new tunnel is being drilled with the same length, but twice the diameter. How many cubic meters of rock and dirt will be drilled from the new tunnel?

A. 635,850 m^3

B. 1,271,700 m^3

C. 1,695,600 m^3

D. 2,543,400 m^3

81. Given that $f(x) = 6x - 21$ and $g(x) = x^3 - 7x$, determine $(g \circ f)(3)$.

  A. -15

  B. 6

  C. -6

  D. 15

82. What is the first step in simplifying the following problem?

$$2\left(\frac{-11}{5\sqrt{\frac{76}{49}}}\right)^{-4}$$

  A. Square -4.

  B. Find the square root of $\frac{76}{49}$.

  C. Multiply 2 and -11.

  D. Divide -11 by 5.

83. If $x_1 = 7$, $y_1 = 9$ and y varies directly as x, find the constant of variation k.

  A. 1.286

  B. 4.5

  C. 16

  D. 30.1

84. In how many ways can Emma arrange 3 dolls, 5 trucks, and 4 teddy bears?

  A. $\dfrac{12!}{12}$

  B. $\dfrac{12!}{5! \times 4! \times 3!}$

  C. $12!$

  D. $5! + 4! + 3!$

85. A particular plumbing job takes $7\frac{1}{2}$ hours to complete. Plumber A charges $30 dollars an hour to do the work. Plumber B charges $42.50 per hour. What is difference between what the plumbers will charge for the work?

  A. $60.50

  B. $109.25

  C. $76.00

  D. $93.75

86. Find x.

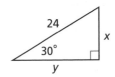

  A. 24

  B. 12

  C. $24\sqrt{3}$

  D. $12\sqrt{3}$

87. Line r is tangent to circle B at T. $BT = 2$, $BS = 1$, and $WT = 5$. Find BA.

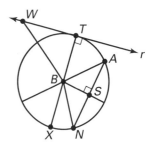

  A. 1

  B. 5

  C. 2

  D. 7

Sample Test A Grade 11

Name_____ Date _____ Class_____

88. Which points are greater than $\frac{35}{5}$?

A. Only T, R
B. Only H, M
C. Only K
D. Only H, K, M

89. Which expression represents the verbal phrase "four less than seven times the quantity of a number and five"?

A. $4(7n + 5)$
B. $7(n + 5) - 4$
C. $5 + n \cdot 7 \cdot 4$
D. $5 + (n + 7)$

90. A solid has 6 congruent square faces. What is the solid?

A. triangular prism
B. rectangular prism
C. cube
D. pyramid

91. A 45°-45°-90° triangle has a leg that is 5 cm. Find the approximate length of the longer leg.

A. 3.5 cm
B. 5 cm
C. 7.8 cm
D. 10 cm

92. Determine the surface are of a hemisphere with radius 10.5 ft. (Round to the nearest hundredth if necessary.)

A. 489.05 ft^2
B. 692.72 ft^2
C. 1385.44 ft^2
D. 2424.50 ft^2

Gridded-Response: Fill in the grid with your answer to each question.

93. As a short cut, Louise walks diagonally through a rectangular parking lot that measures 42 m by 60 m. John walks the length and the width of the parking lot. How much farther, in meters, does John walk than Louise? Round the answer to the nearest hundredth.

94. In order for the polynomial, $x^2 - 5x + c$, to be a perfect square trinomial, what is the value of c? Write your answer as a decimal.

95. What is the probability of rolling a sum of 2 or a sum of 8? Round your answer to the nearest percent.

(1,1)	(1,2)	(1,3)	(1,4)	(1,5)	(1,6)
(2,1)	(2,2)	(2,3)	(2,4)	(2,5)	(2,6)
(3,1)	(3,2)	(3,3)	(3,4)	(3,5)	(3,6)
(4,1)	(4,2)	(4,3)	(4,4)	(4,5)	(4,6)
(5,1)	(5,2)	(5,3)	(5,)4	(5,5)	(5,6)
(6,1)	(6,2)	(6,3)	(6,4)	(6,5)	(6,6)

Sample Test A Grade 11

Name_____ Date _____ Class_____

Extended-Response: Show your work for each question.

96. One side of an isosceles triangle is 2.6 m long. What must be true about the lengths of the other two sides? Explain.

97. You are shopping for a costume. The sales tax is 8.25%. You have a total of $58 to spend.

   A. Write and solve an inequality to determine the price limit for the costume. Explain how you got this answer.

   B. If the price is $55, what is the highest tax rate that can be put on the costume for you to be able to afford it? Explain your answer.

98. Melissa's brother is seven years less than twice her age. The sum of her age and her brother's age is 28. Write an equation that best shows this information.

99. In $\triangle ABC$, m$\angle B = 90°$, m$\angle A = 34°$, and $b = 14$ cm. Which of the other two sides of the triangle is longer? How much longer?

100. A baseball player's batting statistics are given.

Outcome	Experimental Probability	Outcome	Experimental Probability
Single	0.198	Ground out	0.164
Double	0.161	Fly out	0.087
Triple	0.120	Strike out	0.020
Home Run	0.132	Sacrifce	0.060
Walk	0.018	Bunt	0.040
		Total	1.00

   A. If a batter is up to bat 5 times during one game, how many times will he strike out, ground out, fly out, or sacrifice?

   B. If a batter is up to bat 23 times in one month, how many times will the player hit a home run?

Sample Test A Grade 11

SAMPLE TEST B

Select the best answer for each question.

1. Solve the system below and determine the value of $2x - y$.

$$3x + 4y = 65$$
$$\frac{1}{14}x - y = -10\frac{1}{2}$$

A. 0

B. 2

C. 3

D. $4\frac{1}{2}$

2. The two numbers that are 5 units from 3 on a number line are represented by the absolute-value equation $|n - 3| = 5$. What are these two numbers?

A. −8, 2

B. 5, −7

C 7, −5

D. 8, −2

3. Marianne is doing a word problem that says the sum of three consecutive even numbers is 42. She sets up the expression:

$$n + (n + 2) + (n + 4) = 42$$

Is this right?

A. Yes

B. No

C. Cannot determine

D. None of the above

4. What information could be added to the table in order for a line graph to be a more appropriate graphical representation of the data?

Fruit	Day 1	Day 2
Bananas	16	22
Kiwi	8	6
Mango	24	18
Oranges	40	50
Apples	52	50

A. The number of watermelon sold during the two days.

B. The total number of fruit sold at the end of each day.

C. The number of fruit sold on days 3, 4, and 5.

D. The median number of fruit sold.

5. Jean wrote the possible readings on the speedometer of her new car in set-builder notation. Which of the following could be the set she wrote?

A. $\{x \mid 0 > x > 120\}$

B. $\{x \mid x = 10n, n \le 12\}$

C. $\{10, 20, 30, 40, 50 \dots 120\}$

D. $\{x \mid 0 \le x \le 120\}$

6. The length of the diagonal of one of the bases of a cube is $15\sqrt{2}$ inches. What is the surface area of the cube?

A. 180 square inches

B. 225 square inches

C. 1080 square inches

D. 1350 square inches

7. A new school was asked to determine its mascot. The school had 5 choices: grizzly bear, bull dog, bald eagle, wildcat, or panther. The students were polled by the school newspaper as to which mascot they would vote for. The table shows the results of the poll. What is the probability that a student will not vote for the mascot to be a grizzly bear?

Mascot	Number of Votes
Grizzly Bear	68
Bull Dog	12
Bald Eagle	24
Wildcat	44
Panther	52

A. $\dfrac{3}{50}$ **C.** $\dfrac{13}{50}$

B. $\dfrac{11}{50}$ **D.** $\dfrac{33}{50}$

8. Which of the following is not an exponential function?

A. $f(x) = 2^x$

B. $f(x) = \left(\dfrac{7}{2}\right)^x + 6$

C. $f(x) = 3(x)^{5-2} + 5$

D. All of the above are exponential functions.

9. Three coordinates of a parallelogram *ABCD* are $A(-2, 1)$, $C(1, -1)$, and $D(-5, -1)$. Which coordinates could represent point *B*?

A. $(-3, 6)$

B. $(-3, 3)$

C. $(-1, -5)$

D. $(4, 1)$

10. What is the volume of the cube shown below?

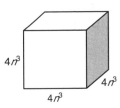

A. $12n^6$ in^3

B. $12n^9$ in^3

C. $64n^9$ in^3

D. $256n^9$ in^3

11. Factoring $100x^2 - 36y^2$ will result in:

A. $(10x - 6y)(10x + 6y)$

B. $(15x + 3y)(15x - 3y)$

C. $(50x - 3y)(50x - y)$

D. $2(5x - 3y)(5x + 3y)$

12. Determine the circumference of a semicircle that has a radius of 1.7 cm. (Use 3.14 for π)

A. 1.45 cm

B. 4.54 cm

C. 8.738 cm

D. 14.08 cm

13. The monthly water temperatures in degrees Fahrenheit for the last 12 months in St. Petersburg, Florida are given below. What is the standard deviation for the data?

Jan	Feb	Mar	Apr	May	Jun
62°	64°	68°	74°	80°	84°

Jul	Aug	Sep	Oct	Nov	Dec
86°	86°	84°	78°	70°	64°

A. 8.8   **C.** 12.3

B. 9.6   **D.** 15

14. The slope of a line is the GCF of 48 and 12. The y-intercept is the GCF of the slope and 8. Which equation describes the line?

A. $y = 12x + 4$

B. $y = 6x + 2$

C. $y = 4x + 4$

D. $y = 3x + 1$

15. What is $f(2)$ in the following equation?

$$f(x) = 10x + 8$$

A. 4

B. 11

C. 17

D. 28

16. A ladder is 3.5 m long. It is leaning against a wall. The foot of the ladder is 1.0 m from the base of the wall. What is the angle between the ladder and the ground? Give your answer to the nearest tenth of a degree.

A. 73.4

B. 87

C. 90

D. 119.4

17. Solve for t given that $7 = \sqrt{6t + 13}$.

A. −4.5

B. 3

C. 6

D. 21.33

18. Each month, Mrs. Li pays her phone company $28 for phone service and $0.07 per minute for long distance calls. Which expression represents her bill for a month in which long distance calls totaled 4 hours?

A. $4[28 + 60(0.07)]$

B. $28 + 0.07 + 4$

C. $28 + 0.07(4)$

D. $28 + 4(60)(0.07)$

19. Suppose point $A(7, -2)$ is translated by the following rule.
$(x, y) \rightarrow (x - 5, y + 4)$. What are the coordinates of A'?

A. $(2, -2)$

B. $(2, 2)$

C. $(12, -2)$

D. $(12, 2)$

20. What is the pattern?

$$4, -16, 64, -256, \ldots$$

A. Multiply by 4.

B. Multiply by −4.

C. Divide by −0.4.

D. None of the above.

21. A lunch check for Mark and a friend was $19.50 before the 6% sales tax was added. Mark wants to leave a tip of at least 20%. What is the least amount he should leave to pay the check, tax, and tip?

A. $13.45

B. $17.60

C. $24.57

D. $27.25

Sample Test B Grade 11

22. What is $(3xy)^2$ in simplified form?

    A. $9x^2y^3$

    B. $9x^2y^2$

    C. $9x^3y^2$

    D. None of the above

23. Which statement is ALWAYS true for the angles formed by parallel lines and a transversal?

    A. Same-side interior angles are equal

    B. Alternate angles are equal

    C. Corresponding angles are supplementary

    D. All of these statements are always true

24. What is the minimum number of roots a 3rd degree polynomial function can have?

    A. 0

    B. 1

    C. 2

    D. 3

25. A radio station surveyed its listeners to determine the ages of its listeners. The results are shown below in the stem-and-leaf plot.

Stem	Leaf (Key: 3|2 = 32)
0	8 8 9
1	0 1 3 4 4 6 6 8 8 9
2	0 0 0 4 8 9
3	2 3 4 5 6 6 8 9 9
4	4 5
5	2 7 9
6	1 2 8

Which numbers can be used to determine the median of the data?

    A. 20, 20   **C.** 24, 28

    B. 8, 68   **D.** 28, 29

26. Which of the following is false?

    A A quadratic equation can always be solved using the quadratic formula.

    B Given 2 roots, I can write out a quadratic equation.

    C Roots help us to graph the equation.

    D The term containing x^2 will have a negative coefficient if the parabola opens down.

27. $f(x) = x^2 + 5$ and $g(x) = -f(x)$. How are they related?

    A. They have the same graph.

    B. Their graphs are vertical reflections of each other.

    C. Their graphs are horizontal reflections of each other.

    D. Their graphs are vertical shifts of each other.

Sample Test B Grade 11

28. Which statement is a counterexample for the following conjecture?

The square root of a whole number is a rational number.

   A. The square roots of some numbers are whole numbers.

   B. The square root of 2 is a non-terminating, non-repeating decimal; this is an irrational number.

   C. Taking a square root is the opposite operation to squaring.

   D. Fractions, integers, and decimals that terminate or repeat are rational numbers.

29. Which set of line segments would not form a triangle?

   A. 21 cm, 32 cm, 63 cm

   B. 29 cm, 38 cm, 12 cm

   C. 44 cm, 55 cm, 66 cm

   D. 67 cm, 36 cm, 41 cm

30. Given $2y - x = 4x + 2 - 3y$, what is the slope of the line?

   A. 1

   B. 2

   C. 3

   D. 4

31. Solve for x.

$$\frac{8(x - 1)}{x^2 - 4} = \frac{4}{x - 2}$$

   A. 4

   B. 6

   C. 8

   D. 12

32. Each square represents a probability of 0.02. The squares with A represent the probability that event A occurs. The Z represents the probability that event Z occurs. The area where the two letters overlap represents the probability that both events occur.

A	A	A	A	A
	A	A	A	Z
	Z	Z	Z	Z
A	A	A	Z	Z
A	Z	Z	Z	A
AZ	AZ	A	AZ	A
AZ	AZ	AZ	Z	Z
A	A	Z	Z	AZ
AZ		A	Z	AZ
A	Z	AZ	A	AZ

What is the probability that neither event A nor event Z occurs?

   A. 0.02

   B. 0.06

   C. 0.6

   D. 1

33. A quality control inspector has found that 3.2% of the garments produced at Standard Garments contain a defect. If Standard Garments produces 4117 garments per day, about how many total garments are expected to have a defect during a 7-day week?

   A. 132

   B. 321

   C. 922

   D. 1045

34. There are about 3.2×10^7 seconds in one year. What is this number in standard form?

- **A.** 0.000000032
- **B.** 0.00000032
- **C.** 32,000,000
- **D.** 320,000,000

35. The dollar amount of the total purchases from a corner kiosk over a 3-month period is shown below for 21 randomly selected individuals.

$10	$18	$10	$22	$14	$41	$31
$43	$8	$6	$27	$18	$27	$32
$5	$53	$30	$25	$30	$22	$42

Find the median of the dollar amounts.

- **A.** $15.00
- **B.** $18.50
- **C.** $25.00
- **D.** $31.25

36. The length of a rectangle is 13 more than the width. If the length of the diagonal is 65 units, what is the area of the rectangle?

- **A.** 39 square units
- **B.** 52 square units
- **C.** 1521 square units
- **D.** 2028 square units

37. Solve for x:

$$\frac{3}{4}\left(\frac{4}{5}x - 2\right) = \frac{11}{4}$$

- **A.** $\frac{17}{12}$
- **B.** $\frac{19}{12}$
- **C.** $\frac{85}{12}$
- **D.** 4

38. Jill invests $12,500 in stocks and savings bonds. The money in stocks earns 5% interest while the money in savings bonds earns 3% interest. If Jill wants to earn $431 in interest, how much money should she invest in stocks?

- **A.** $1250.50
- **B.** $1750.00
- **C.** $2245.00
- **D.** $2800.00

39. What is the equation of a line that passes through $(-6, 8)$ and is parallel to the x-axis?

- **A.** $y = -6$
- **B.** $y = -4$
- **C.** $y = 0$
- **D.** $y = 8$

40. What is the exponent on the x-term after the expression below is simplified?

$$x^{\frac{3}{2}}\left(\sqrt{x^3}\right)^4$$

- **A.** -2
- **B.** 2.5
- **C.** $\frac{15}{2}$
- **D.** 15

Sample Test B Grade 11

41. A card is drawn from a deck of 52 playing cards. What is the probability of drawing a queen or a spade?

A. $\frac{1}{13}$ **C.** $\frac{4}{13}$

B. $\frac{2}{13}$ **D** $\frac{8}{13}$

42. Which set best describes the numbers graphed on the number line?

$$-3 \ -2 \ -1 \quad 0 \quad 1 \quad 2 \quad 3$$

A. $\{-6.3, -1.\overline{3}, \frac{3}{4}, \sqrt{2}\}$

B. $\{-2, -1, |5|, 0.5, 1.5\}$

C. $\{-1\frac{1}{3}, 0.\overline{3}, 1.5, 2\}$

D. $\{-2, -\frac{5}{3}, 0.3333, 1.5\}$

43. What is the growth factor of $f(x) = (2^2 + 3)^x (6)$?

A. 2

B. 3

C. 7

D 6

44. What is the common factor of the two functions below?

$$f(x) = x^2 + 7x + 12$$

$$g(x) = -2x^2 - 7x - 3$$

A. $x + 3$

B. $x - 3$

C. $x + 4$

D. $x - 4$

45. A man starts at point A and walks 7 miles east on a straight path to point B. Point C is directly north of point A. The straight path from A to C and the straight path from B to C form an angle of 37° at point C. The man wants to walk from B to C. Which diagram models this problem?

A.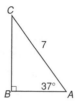

C.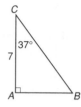

B.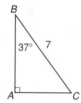

D.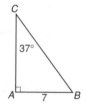

46. A manager at Cheap Cars Store recorded the number of cars sold each day for two weeks. The data set is as follows:

4, 8, 10, 3, 7, 8, 0, 13, 43, 5, 2, 9, 8, 6

Out of the following, which value is the largest for this data set?

A. Mean   **C.** Mode

B. Median   **D.** Range

47. In the table what is the value of n?

x	0	1	2	3
y	25	30	n	40

A. 32

B. 35

C. 37.5

D. none of the above

48. A health club charges a $675 membership fee per year, this includes 5 free guest passes. Each guest pass above 5 costs $8.00. You have determined that the function $t = 675 + 8(g - 5)$ will model the yearly cost. How much will it cost if you take 8 guests to the health club?

    A. $500.00

    B. $699.00

    C. $725.50

    D. $890.00

49. Anthony had 10 packages of markers. Each package contained 8 markers. He gave his 3 best friends 2 packages each. Which expression shows how many markers he kept for himself?

    A. $8(10 - 3 \times 2)$

    B. $8(10 + 3 \times 2)$

    C. $10 \times 6 - 10 \times 3 \times 2$

    D. $10 \times 8 - 3 \times 2$

50. In a parallelogram, how are opposite interior angles related?

    A. they are equal

    B. they are supplementary

    C. they are complementary

    D. they are not related

51. Simplify $(x + 1)^2$.

    A. $2x + 1$

    B. $x^2 + 1$

    C. 1

    D. None of the above

52. Two hundred patrons were asked about their favorite features of Big Meal Restaurants. The results are shown in the circle graph.

Features of Big Meal Restaurant

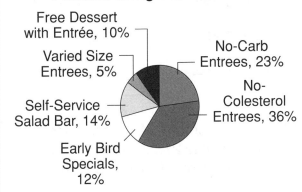

Which category has one-third of the number of patrons as those who liked the No-Cholesterol Entrees?

    A. Early Bird Specials

    B. Self-Service Salad Bar

    C Varied Size Entrees

    D. No-Carb Entrees

53. The interior angles of a triangle measure 88°, 34°, and 58°. Which type of triangle is it?

    A. Acute scalene triangle

    B. Obtuse isosceles triangle

    C. Acute isosceles triangle

    D. Obtuse scalene triangle

Sample Test B Grade 11

54. What are the roots for the equation?

$$y = 6x^2 + 5x - 4$$

A. $-\dfrac{4}{3}$ and $-\dfrac{1}{2}$

B. $-\dfrac{4}{3}$ and $\dfrac{1}{2}$

C. $\dfrac{4}{3}$ and $-\dfrac{1}{2}$

D. $\dfrac{4}{3}$ and $\dfrac{1}{2}$

55. The temperature of the core of the Sun reaches 27,720,000°F. What is this temperature written in scientific notation?

A. 2.7×10^7

B. 2.72×10^7

C. 2.772×10^7

D. 2.772×10^8

56. Which of the following BEST represents the value of x in this inequality?

$$2x + 4 > 12$$

A. $x > 4$

B. $x > -4$

C. $x < -4$

D. $x < 4$

57. If the side length of a cube is 16 in., what is the length of the diagonal shown? Write your answer in simplest radical form.

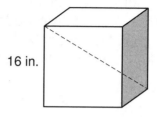

16 in.

A. $16\sqrt{2}$ in.

B. $16\sqrt{3}$ in.

C. 256 in.

D. 512 in.

58. Katy likes to catch butterflies. The equation $b = 3(x - 7)^2 + 11$ models this habit, where b is the number of butterflies caught for the hour and x is the number of hours after she started catching. She will catch the maximum amount per hour after ___ hours.

A. 11

B. 7

C. 3

D. None of the above, it is a flawed model.

59. The local baseball pitcher has made the following number of strikeouts in the past 9 starts:

11, 3, 4, 10, 12, 5, 7, 13, 4

How many must he get in his next start to average 8 for the season?

A. 4

B. 7

C. 8

D. 11

Sample Test B Grade 11

60. Solve for t given that $7 = \sqrt{6t + 13}$.

  A. −4.5

  B. 3

  C. 6

  D. 21.33

61. There are 12 blocks in a bag. There are 4 red blocks, 4 green blocks, and 4 blue blocks. You pick out three blocks. Each time a block is picked, it is not replaced back into the bag. What is the probability of choosing a red block, then a green block, and finally a blue block?

  A. $\dfrac{1}{330}$

  B. $\dfrac{8}{165}$

  C. $\dfrac{12}{33}$

  D. $\dfrac{1}{27}$

62. An angle measures 18°. What is the measure of a supplementary angle?

  A. 72°

  B. 82°

  C. 162°

  D. 342°

63. The circumference of a circular animal pen is 42.7 meters. What is the radius of the pen, to the nearest tenth of a meter?

  A. 2.1 m

  B. 3.4 m

  C. 6.8 m

  D. 13.6 m

64. A standard six-sided die is rolled twice. What is the probability of getting a sum of 7?

  A. $\dfrac{1}{3}$

  B. $\dfrac{1}{4}$

  C. $\dfrac{1}{5}$

  D. $\dfrac{1}{6}$

65. A famous natural designer plans to create a garden around the town's oldest tree. He wants to center a square around the tree to protect it. Each side of the square will be 26 feet long. The garden will be a circle centered around the square. The area of the garden should be 33,286 square feet, NOT including the area of the square.

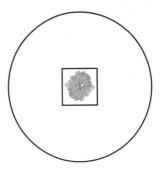

The designer is planning to put a brick walkway around the edge of the circular garden. How long should the walkway be?

  A. 60 feet

  B. 640 feet

  C. 653 feet

  D. 682 feet

Sample Test B Grade 11

66. The table below shows the populations of several countries.

Country	Population
Mexico	106,202,903
Canada	32,805,041
Belgium	10,364,388
Australia	20,090,437
Russia	143,420,309

If $\frac{1}{5}$ of the population of Canada owns a pet, estimate using benchmarks the number of people who own a pet.

A. 6,600,000

B. 6,500,000

C. 7,000,000

D. 6,780,000

67. Does the following statement represent a linear function?

A swimming pool charges a $75 membership fee per year, and $1.50 each time you bring a guest. Which expression shows the yearly cost y in terms of the number of guests g?

A. Yes

B. No, it should be quadratic

C. No, it should be cubic

D. No, it should be exponential

68. Given the constant of variation k is 0.5, what will be the value for y if $x = 0.2$ and if x and y are inversely related?

A. 2.5

B. 1

C. 3

D. 12

69. Do quadratic functions always have a degree 2?

A. Yes

B. No

C. Sometimes

D. It cannot be determined.

70. In a track meet, 10 runners compete for first, second, and third place. How many different ways can the runners place if there are no ties?

A. 24

B. 450

C. 720

D. 1000

71. What is the absolute value of the difference of the expression

$$\frac{2^3 + 4^2 + x\sqrt{169}}{5^2}, \text{ when } x = 0 \text{ and}$$

when $x = 1$?

A. 1.48

B. 1.00

C. 0.96

D. 0.52

72. Will a smaller base guarantee that an exponential function will increase more slowly than a function with a larger base?

A. Yes

B. No

C. Sometimes

D. Cannot be determined

73. About how many 12-ounce paper cups can Rico fill with a 1.75-liter container of water?
28.6 milliliters ≈ 1 fluid ounce

A. 5 cups

B. 6 cups

C. 7 cups

D. 9 cups

74. The ordered pairs shown form a pattern.

x	y
0	0
1	1
2	8
3	27
4	64
5	??

What is the missing y-value?

A. 95

B. 125

C. 75

D. 251

75. A construction company paves about 1.5 kilometers of highway per day. If there are 30 days in a month, about how many kilometers of highway will be paved by the end of the month?

A. 205 kilometers

B. 45 kilometers

C. 20,000 kilometers

D. 45,000 kilometers

76. Mr. and Mrs. Watson compare 2 home blueprints when building a house. The first house is 3650 square feet with 8 ft walls. The second house is 2650 square feet with 9.5 ft walls. How many more cubic feet of air do the furnace and air conditioner need to warm and cool the first house than the second?

A. 1100 cubic feet

B. 3150 cubic feet

C. 4025 cubic feet

D. 4850 cubic feet

77. Line r is tangent to circle B at T. $BT = 2$, $BS = 1$, and $WT = 5$. Find SN.

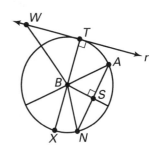

A. About 1.2

B. About 1.7

C. About 2.2

D. About 2.9

78. The distance from Earth to the moon is 22^4 mi. The distance from Earth to Neptune is about 22^7 mi. How many one-way trips from Earth to the moon are equal to 1 trip from Earth to Neptune?

A. 3

B. 10^3

C. 32^2

D. 22^3

Sample Test B Grade 11

79. A rubber ball has a diameter of 6 inches. If a basketball has a diameter of three times as large, determine the surface area of the basketball. (Use $\pi = 3.14$, round to the nearest hundredth if necessary.)

A. 452.16 in^2

B. 1017.36 in^2

C. 226.08 in^2

D. 524.16 in^2

80. Find the median of the data below.

2, 4, 5, 7, 9, 11, 17, 22, 37, 57, 69

A. 2

B. 11

C. 22

D. 33

81. Simplify.

$$\frac{3\left(\sqrt[3]{\frac{(-2)^2}{9}}\right)^3}{-2}$$

A. $-\frac{8}{3}$

B. $-\frac{2}{3}$

C. $-\frac{5}{6}$

D. $\frac{13}{6}$

82. The ratio of the corresponding sides of two similar triangles is 4:9. The sides of the smaller triangle are 20 cm, 32 cm, and 36 cm. Find the perimeter of the larger triangle.

A. 792 cm

B. 352 cm

C. 198 cm

D. 88 cm

83. What is the difference of the absolute value of the expression $4x^2 - 6x + 4$, when $x = 0$ and when $x = 1$?

A. 4

B. 3

C. 2

D. 1

Gridded-Response: Fill in the grid with your answer to each question.

84. A walkway is created to connect the opposite corners of a public park. If the width of the park is 148 m and the area of the park is 29,896 m^2, what is the length of the walkway? Round your answers to the nearest hundredth.

Sample Test B Grade 11

Name_____ Date _____ Class_____

Extended-Response: Show your work for each question.

85. Is the following situation dependent or independent? Amy chooses a card from a deck of cards. Luke chooses a card from the same deck. The person with the highest card goes first in their game of crazy eights.

86. The average speed for the winner of the 2002 Indianapolis 500 was 25 mi/h greater than the average speed for the 2001 winner. In addition, the 2002 winner completed the 500 mi race 32 min faster than the 2001 winner. Let s represent the average speed of the 2001 winner in miles per hour.

  A. Write expressions in terms of s for the time in hours that it took the 2001 and 2002 winners to complete the race.

  B. Write a rational equation that can be used to determine s. Solve your equation to find the average speed of the 2001 winner to the nearest mile per hour.

87. These are the heights, in inches, of the players on the high school basketball team.

  72 75 60 72 71 70 72 73 70 74

  A. What is the outlier in this data set? Explain why it is an outlier?

  B. What effect does removing this value have on the mean and the standard deviation? Explain your answer and show your work.

88. Marianne is doing a word problem that says the sum of three numbers is 648. These numbers are consecutively increasing multiples of 3. The equation that she sets up is
$k + (k + 3) + (k + 6) = 225$.
What does the variable k represent?

89. The length of a rectangle is double the width. The area of the rectangle is 84.5 m^2. What are the dimensions of the rectangle?

Sample Test B Grade 11